15 FUTURE EVENTS
THAT WILL
SHAKE
THE WORLD

ED HINDSON

HARVEST HOUSE PUBLISHERS
EUGENE, OREGON

Cover by Dugan Design Group, Bloomington, Minnesota

Cover photo © Shutterstock / Igor Zh.

15 FUTURE EVENTS THAT WILL SHAKE THE WORLD
Copyright © 2014 by Ed Hindson
Published by Harvest House Publishers
Eugene, Oregon 97402
www.harvesthousepublishers.com

Library of Congress Cataloging-in-Publication Data
Hindson, Edward E.
 15 future events that will shake the world / Ed Hindson.
    pages cm
Includes bibliographical references.
ISBN 978-0-7369-5308-5 (pbk.)
ISBN 978-0-7369-5309-2 (eBook)
 1. End of the world—Biblical teaching. 2. Bible—Prophecies—End of the world. I. Title. II. Title: Fifteen future events that will shake the world
BS649.E63H555 2014
236'.9—dc23

2013045507

Printed in the United States of America

21 22 / VP-JH / 11 10

With special thanks to
Dillon Burroughs
and
Michael W. Herbert
Editorial Assistants

And there shall be signs in the sun, and in the moon, and in the stars...for the powers of heaven shall be shaken...and when these things begin to come to pass, then look up, and lift up your heads; for your redemption draweth nigh.

LUKE 21:25-28

CONTENTS

INTRODUCTION

What can people on earth expect during the last days? In all the chaos that the Bible predicts, several events stand out as truly extraordinary—so much so that they arouse many questions from Christians and non-Christians alike.

What are these events, and what makes them so significant? Jesus warned that a time would come when God would literally shake the world. The heavens and the earth would be shaken. Stunning events in the future would affect life on earth.

In part 1 we'll look at "Seven Future Events That Will Shake the World." In part 2 we'll examine "Five Signs That Reveal the Future." Then we'll conclude with part 3, "Three Prophecies That Prove the Bible Is True." You'll discover information regarding...

- millions missing in the rapture
- power shifts in the USA and the rest of the world after the rapture
- the rise of a global dictator
- God's two witnesses rising from the dead in plain view
- the rebuilt Jewish temple usurped by the Antichrist
- the Holocaust eclipsed
- Christ's glorious return to earth as Conqueror and King

This book will give you a clear overview of world events—how they will unfold, what they mean to us, and God's purposes for bringing them about in the days ahead.

Bible prophecy is not written to scare us. It is written to prepare us. God's Word reveals these future events to assure us that He is in control even when the world appears to be out of control. His predictions about the future remind us to keep watching and be ready for the Lord's return, even as Jesus urged us (Matthew 24:42,44).

Those of us who take the Bible seriously live with an eye on the sky but our feet on the earth. We believe the promise of the imminent return of Christ, but we also clearly understand our God-given responsibility to make a difference in this world to the glory of God. Therefore we keep looking up as we continue marching on.

Looking for that blessed hope, and the glorious appearing
of the great God and our Savior Jesus Christ...

Titus 2:13

PART 1

SEVEN FUTURE EVENTS
THAT WILL SHAKE THE WORLD

Today's world already presents enormous challenges, yet the Bible predicts seven future events that will shake the world beyond anything it has ever known. A coming disappearance of millions of people will change the axis of power across the globe. The United States will diminish as the world's largest superpower in a single day. A new global leader will announce a plan for world peace.

In the midst of this global upheaval, the world will experience a truly miraculous scenario—the resurrection of two men who had been dead three days. A new Jewish temple will be completed on the Temple Mount, likely in the wake of a destroyed Dome of the Rock. Another Jewish Holocaust—this one greater than that perpetrated by the Nazi regime—will lead to an intense series of judgments until Jesus Himself returns to earth.

The prophet Isaiah foresaw these devastating scenarios.

> The floodgates of the heavens are opened,
>   the foundations of the earth shake.
> The earth is broken up,
>   the earth is split asunder,
>   the earth is violently shaken.
> The earth reels like a drunkard,
>   it sways like a hut in the wind;
> so heavy upon it is the guilt of its rebellion
>   that it falls—never to rise again
>   (Isaiah 24:18-20 NIV).

Jesus Himself predicted that amazing cosmic events would occur.

> And there shall be signs in the sun, and in the moon, and in the stars…distress of nations…men's hearts failing them for fear…for the powers of heaven shall be shaken…and when these things begin to come to pass, then look up, and lift your heads; for your redemption draweth nigh (Luke 21:25-28).

What will these earthshaking events be? When will they occur? What can we do to be prepared?

1

MILLIONS MISSING

The tragic events of 9/11 produced a time of mourning unprecedented in recent American society. Nearly 3000 lives were lost in one day. The Twin Towers—symbols of American economic power—collapsed. The Pentagon sustained significant damage.

News outlets played and replayed the horrific events and eyewitness accounts for weeks. Still today, years removed from 9/11, we remember the lives lost on that fateful day and promise to never forget.

Amazingly, the Bible predicts a tragedy on a much larger scale in the days ahead. Jesus warned that in the future, God will literally shake the heavens and the earth. And one day, millions of people will be missing—unexpectedly, instantly, without warning, and without any signs. The Bible tells us that suddenly the Spirit of God will move, the trumpet will sound, the archangel will shout, and Christ will come and rapture believers home to heaven.

Those of us who are believers look forward to this event as the blessed hope that Jesus is coming again to take us home to the Father's house. But this will be a terrible time for those who are left behind on the earth. Think of the effect it will have on the economy, the government, the stability of society, and the family members and loved ones who turn around and suddenly realize somebody is not there, with no explanation of where they have gone. The Bible clearly describes this event.

> But I would not have you to be ignorant, brethren, concerning them which are asleep, that ye sorrow not, even

as others which have no hope. For if we believe that Jesus
died and rose again, even so them also which sleep in
Jesus will God bring with him (1 Thessalonians 4:13-14).

When believers die, their bodies go to the grave and their spirits go to heaven. At the time of the rapture, these spirits will return
from heaven with Christ. Their bodies will be resurrected and
reunited with their spirits, and then we will literally be taken, body
and spirit, home to the Father's house. Paul continues describing
this amazing event.

> This we say unto you by the word of the Lord, that we
> which are alive and remain unto the coming of the Lord
> shall not prevent them which are asleep. For the Lord
> himself shall descend from heaven with a shout, with the
> voice of the archangel, and with the trump of God: and
> the dead in Christ shall rise first: then we which are alive
> and remain shall be caught up together with them in the
> clouds, to meet the Lord in the air: and so shall we ever
> be with the Lord. Wherefore comfort one another with
> these words (verses 15-18).

Here is a message of comfort and encouragement for the believer.
Jesus said to the disciples on the last night before He suffered on the
cross, "I go to prepare a place for you. And if I go and prepare a place
for you, I will come again, and receive you unto myself; that where
I am, there ye may be also" (John 14:2-3). That is the promise of
the rapture, when believers are "caught up," as the King James Ver-
sion says. Suddenly we will be snatched away to be with our Savior.

I know that people have a lot of questions about what will happen at the time of the rapture. If we are raptured, what will happen
to our clothes? Will we ascend clothes and all? My friend Dr. Tim
LaHaye suggests your clothes will be left behind as a testimony to
the fact that you have been raptured. There is no clear evidence in
the Bible one way or the other, but the question opens the door to

other interesting questions. What about eyeglasses? Contacts? What about false teeth or artificial parts? Some people would have more left behind than taken!

We don't know some of the details, but the big picture of Bible prophecy is always clear—one day the Lord is coming for His own. That is why Jesus said, "Keep watch, because you do not know on what day your Lord will come…So you also must be ready" (Matthew 24:42,44 NIV). "It's like a man going away: He leaves his house and puts his servants in charge, each with their assigned task, and tells the one at the door to keep watch" (Mark 13:34 NIV).

This first shocking event that will shake the world in the future is the rapture of the church, when believers are suddenly missing from every nation in the world. The population of the entire planet will be stunned. Yet the Bible tells us those left behind will believe a lie about what has happened. I don't know what that lie will be—it may have to do with aliens or some other unprovable scenario. Those left behind may promise, "Don't worry, we'll find them." Some kind of explanation will be given. But the truth is, the rapture will change everything.

What Is the Rapture?

We've mentioned the rapture, but what does the Bible teach that the rapture is? The Bible clearly teaches that a time is coming when Christ will return for His own. We looked at 1 Thessalonians 4:15-18 above. This passage of Scripture mentions five stages to the rapture:

1. The Lord Himself will descend from heaven with a shout and with the sound of a trumpet.
2. The dead in Christ will rise first.
3. Then we who are alive and remain on earth will be caught up together with them in the clouds.
4. We will meet the Lord in the air.
5. And we will always be with Him.

The English word *rapture* comes from the Latin *rapto*, which is a translation of the Greek New Testament word *harpazo*. All these terms mean "caught up" or "snatched away." The word *rapture* does not appear in English translations, but the concept of the rapture certainly does. The rapture will occur suddenly, instantaneously, and without warning.

The apostle Paul also unveiled what he referred to as a mystery pertaining to the rapture. He explained that some Christians will not sleep, or die. Instead, their bodies will be instantly transformed.

> Behold, I tell you a mystery: We shall not all sleep, but we shall all be changed—in a moment, in the twinkling of an eye, at the last trumpet. For the trumpet will sound, and the dead will be raised incorruptible, and we shall be changed. For this corruptible must put on incorruption, and this mortal must put on immortality (1 Corinthians 15:51-53 NKJV).

At the moment of the rapture, the bodies of all believers who have died with faith in Christ since the Day of Pentecost will suddenly be transformed into new, living, immortal, resurrected bodies. Even bodies that have long since decayed or have been cremated and scattered across the oceans will be made new. These new bodies will be joined together with the people's spirits, which Jesus will bring with Him from heaven. Then the bodies of those who are alive on earth and have accepted Christ as their Savior will also be instantly translated into new, immortal bodies.

Notice the similarity of the descriptions of the rapture in 1 Corinthians 15:51-53 and 2 Thessalonians 4:15-18. When Christ comes to take His church (all believers) to heaven in fulfillment of His promise in John 14:1-3, He will include both the living and the dead.

Together, all believers will be instantaneously transported into heaven to meet their saved loved ones "in the clouds" and then to meet the Lord in the air. Those who have rejected the salvation of

Jesus Christ will remain on earth and witness a miraculous event of astonishing proportions—the sudden mass disappearance of millions upon millions of Christians from the face of the earth.

People often refer to the rapture as the "blessed hope" (Titus 2:13) because it provides comfort not only to those believers who are concerned about the coming tribulations, but also to those who long to be reunited with their departed loved ones who shared their faith in Christ.

The second coming, which encompasses both the rapture (before the tribulation) and the glorious appearing (at the end of the tribulation), is one of the most significant events mentioned in the entire Bible. It is clearly taught in both the Old and New Testaments. The New Testament alone refers to this awesome event 321 times—in one out of every thirty verses—making it the second-most prominent doctrine presented in Scripture after the doctrine of salvation. It is mentioned in every chapter of 1 and 2 Thessalonians, the first books written for the early church. All nine New Testament authors mention the second coming, and 23 of the 27 New Testament books reference it. God clearly intended His church to be motivated to holiness and world evangelism by the study of the second coming of Jesus Christ. Since Jesus is coming again, we are called to live for Christ with urgency and to share Him with everyone we can.

The Phases of the Second Coming

Much confusion exists among Bible readers regarding the second coming of Christ. Of central importance is whether Jesus will return once or twice. I believe it is better to speak of the two phases of the second coming. There are not two second comings. There are two phases to the second coming—the rapture of the church and the return of Christ with the church.

Remember, there were also multiple events related to the first coming of Christ—His birth, life, ministry, death, burial, resurrection, and ascension. These were all parts of the first coming of Christ. Further, there are simply too many conflicting elements in the two phases of His second coming to merge them into a single event. In the first phase, Jesus will come suddenly to rapture His church in the air and take all believers to His Father's house, fulfilling His promise in John 14:1-3. There, they will appear before the judgment seat of Christ (2 Corinthians 5:9-10) and participate in the marriage supper of the Lamb (Revelation 19:1-10).

During this time, those left behind on the earth will experience the trials of the horrendous seven-year tribulation. The apostle Paul distinguishes between the two phases of the second coming in Titus 2:13, where he refers to the rapture as the "blessed hope" and the return of Christ to the earth as the "glorious appearing."

Some theologians attempt to dismiss these multiple phases of Christ's second coming. They place both the rapture and the glorious appearing at the end of the tribulation, and they hold to what is known as the posttribulation view of the rapture. In this scenario, Christians will be required to face the horrors of the tribulation. However, this view teaches that Christ (the bridegroom) will beat up the church (His bride) in order to get her ready for their heavenly marriage!

In order to hold this view, one must ignore numerous passages of Scripture. A careful study of the many biblical references to the second coming clearly shows that the rapture and the glorious appearing are two separate phases of the second coming. Consider the following differences.

The Rapture of the Church	The Glorious Appearing
1. Christ comes *for* believers in the air.	1. Christ comes *with* believers to the earth.
2. All Christians on earth are translated into new bodies.	2. There is no translation of bodies.

3. Christians are taken to the Father's house in heaven.	3. Resurrected saints remain on the earth.
4. There is no judgment on the earth.	4. Christ judges the inhabitants of the earth.
5. The church will be taken to heaven.	5. Christ sets up His kingdom on earth.
6. It could occur anytime (it is imminent).	6. It cannot occur until the end of the seven-year tribulation period.
7. There are no signs preceding it.	7. There are numerous signs preceding it.
8. It affects only believers.	8. It affects all humanity.
9. It is a time of joy.	9. It is a time of mourning.
10. It occurs before the "day of wrath."	10. It occurs after the "day of wrath."
11. Satan is not bound, but wreaks havoc on the earth.	11. Satan is bound in the abyss for 1000 years.
12. Christians are judged at the judgment seat of Christ.	12. Christians have already been judged at the judgment seat.
13. The marriage of the Lamb takes place.	13. The marriage of the Lamb has already taken place.
14. Only Christ's own will see Him.	14. All those on earth will see Him.
15. The seven-year tribulation follows.	15. The 1000-year millennium follows.

When Will the Rapture Occur?

Bible commentators hold various views as to when the rapture will occur (before, during, or after the tribulation), but conservative evangelical commentators agree that there will be a rapture. The only real question is, when will it occur? Christ must return at some point to resurrect the dead in Christ and rapture the living believers in order to take us all to the Father's house in heaven, as Jesus promised in John 14:1-4. Here are seven reasons to believe the rapture will occur before the tribulation begins.

The Lord Himself promised to deliver us. Revelation 3:10 says, "Because you have kept My command to persevere, I also will keep you from the hour of trial which shall come upon the whole world, to test those who dwell on the earth" (NKJV). The Greek word *ek*, which literally means "out of," is translated in this passage as "from." In other words, the Lord intends to keep the church out of the tribulation. Therefore, the rapture must occur before the tribulation begins.

The church is to be delivered from the wrath to come. The apostle Paul tells us in 1 Thessalonians 1:10 that we should "wait for His Son from heaven, whom He raised from the dead, even Jesus who delivers us from the wrath to come" (NKJV). This passage is also referring to the rapture. The church must therefore be removed from the earth before the tribulation begins in order to be delivered from the wrath to come.

The church is not appointed to wrath. According to 1 Thessalonians 5:9, "God did not appoint us to wrath, but to obtain salvation through our Lord Jesus Christ" (NKJV). Once again, the context of these passages is the rapture. The tribulation is prophesied as a time of God's wrath, and Christians are not appointed to wrath, so it follows that the church must be raptured out of the way before the tribulation begins.

The church is absent in Revelation 4–18. Revelation 4–18 details the events of the tribulation. The church is mentioned 17 times in the first three chapters of Revelation, but after John (who is a member of the church) is taken up to heaven at the beginning of chapter 4, the church is not mentioned or seen again until chapter 19, when it appears at the marriage with Christ in heaven and then returns to earth with Jesus at His glorious appearing. Why is the church missing from those chapters? The most likely reason is that the church doesn't go through the tribulation. It will be raptured away before the tribulation begins.

If the church is raptured at the end of the tribulation, there will be no one left to repopulate the earth during the millennium. Just before the millennium begins, all those who have survived the tribulation but still reject Jesus Christ as Savior will be cast into hell (Matthew 25:46). If the rapture occurs at the end of the tribulation, as some believe, all Christians would be taken from the earth as well, leaving no one on earth with a natural body to repopulate the planet during the millennium. The problem here is that numerous Old Testament passages, as well as Revelation 20:7-10, note there will be a huge population explosion during the millennium. Where will these people come from? The best answer is that those who miss the rapture and become believers during the tribulation (thanks to the preaching of the 144,000 Jews and the two witnesses) and survive to the end will repopulate the earth. Many believers will be martyred during the tribulation, but some will survive. These people will not be raptured at the end of the tribulation in some sort of posttribulational rapture, but will instead enter Christ's millennial kingdom with their natural bodies to populate His kingdom. In order for this to be possible, the rapture must take place prior to the tribulation instead of at the end of it.

Only the pretribulational view fulfills Jesus's simple command to "keep watch" and "be ready" until He comes (Matthew 24:42 NIV). He never told us to watch for the Antichrist, the tribulation, or the final judgment. He clearly told His disciples to watch for Him to return and to be ready for Him to come for them.

The rapture before the tribulation fulfills Jesus's promise to take the disciples home to the Father's house in heaven (John 14:2-3). In the upper room, Jesus told His disciples, "I go to prepare a place for you. And if I go and prepare a place for you, I will come again and receive you to Myself; that where I am, there you may be also" (NKJV). Judas had already left the room to betray Jesus. Therefore, he was not a recipient of the rapture promise Jesus affirmed to the 11 believing disciples.

Among the chief features of the rapture is that it will be sudden and will catch people by surprise. "Of that day and hour no one knows" (Matthew 24:36 NKJV), which is why we should live so as to "be ready, for the Son of Man is coming at an hour when you do not expect" (verse 44 NKJV). Only a pretribulation rapture preserves that "any moment" expectation of His coming. Indeed, throughout the ages, the rapture has appeared imminent to Christians of every generation. Nothing could better motivate us to holy living and fervent evangelism than to believe that Jesus could come today. One day He will! The trumpet will sound, the archangel will shout, and we will all go home to be with Jesus.

Raptures in the Bible

God has raptured people to heaven at least three times before.

Enoch. "Enoch walked with God; and he was not, for God took him" (Genesis 5:24). The New Testament adds, "By faith Enoch was taken away so that he did not see death, 'and was not found, because God had taken him'; for before he was taken he had this testimony, that he pleased God" (Hebrews 11:5 NKJV).

Elijah. "Then it happened, as they continued on and talked, that suddenly a chariot of fire appeared with horses of fire, and separated the two of them; and Elijah went up by a whirlwind into heaven" (2 Kings 2:11 NKJV).

Jesus Christ. After His resurrection, Jesus ascended into heaven.

When He had spoken these things, while they watched, He was taken up, and a cloud received Him out of their sight. And while they looked steadfastly toward heaven as He went up, behold, two men stood by them in white apparel, who also said, "Men of Galilee, why do you stand gazing up into heaven? This same Jesus, who was taken up from you into heaven, will so come in like manner as you saw Him go into heaven" (Acts 1:9-11 NKJV).

All three events describe a natural body of flesh being changed and translated into the presence of God. We cannot enter His presence in our finite bodies—a sudden translation is necessary.

The Greek term for the rapture, *harpazo*, is also used in 2 Corinthians 12:2-4, which describes Paul being "caught up" into the third heaven, and in Acts 8:39, which says the Spirit of the Lord "caught away" Phillip after he witnessed to the Ethiopian eunuch. The same term is used of Christ's ascension in Revelation 12:5, where the Bible says the "male child" (Jesus) was "snatched up" (*harpasthe*) to God and his throne. Clearly, the author of Revelation views the ascension as a rapture.

In addition to these, Revelation 11:3-12 also predicts the resurrection and rapture of the two witnesses, who will be martyred during the tribulation. I believe God will use their rapture to assure tribulation saints that the greater rapture had already occurred at the beginning of the tribulation. The rapture of the two witnesses will be a sign of hope to these believers.

The Power of the Rapture

Those in Christ who will be snatched up in the rapture do not have to generate their own power. As in all our dealings with God, He provides the impetus. He has not assigned our resurrection to an angel or any other created being, for "the Lord Himself will descend from heaven with a shout." In other words, He will do the raising. In

John 5:21,28-29, Jesus clearly claimed to possess resurrection power for Himself as proof that He was God in human flesh.

Much is at stake here, including our eternal destiny, so we should notice a most comforting truth. Christ has already demonstrated His power to raise the dead. He did it three times during His brief earthly ministry, the most dramatic of which was when He commanded, "Lazarus, come forth!" (John 11:43). To the astonishment of the people of Bethany, a man dead four days was delivered from his tomb. When that same, experienced voice shouts from heaven at the rapture, all those who are in Christ by faith will respond.

The Lord Jesus Himself declared, "I am the resurrection and the life. He who believes in Me, though he may die, he shall live. And whoever lives and believes in Me shall never die" (John 11:25-26 NKJV). For almost 2000 years, the spirits of all Christians who have died have immediately gone to heaven to be with Christ. Paul said he would be pleased "to be absent from the body, and to be present with the Lord" (2 Corinthians 5:8). When Christ comes for His church, He will resurrect the bodies of deceased saints, unite them with their souls and spirits in heaven, and translate all living believers to be with them and Him forever. No wonder the early Christians used to greet each other with *Maranatha*! ("the Lord is coming").

Many who do not believe in a pretribulational rapture falsely assume there will be no rapture at all. This is a complete misconception. If people take seriously passages like 1 Thessalonians 4:17, "We who are alive and remain shall be caught up together with them in the clouds to meet the Lord in the air" (NASB), they are forced to conclude that there will be a rapture. The only real debate has to do with when it will occur.

Arguments that it is difficult to conceive of millions of people suddenly disappearing are irrelevant. Joking remarks about bumping your head on the ceiling, false teeth being left behind, and hundreds of car accidents suddenly occurring are inconsequential in light of the fact that Scripture clearly states that we will be "caught up" into the air.

There will be a rapture! The only serious questions are, when will it occur, and what is its relationship to the glorious appearing?

The Time of His Coming

Most evangelicals agree as to the nature of Christ's coming, but there is substantial disagreement about the timing. Millard Erickson observes, "The one eschatological doctrine on which orthodox theologians most agree is the second coming of Christ. It is indispensable to eschatology. It is the basis of the Christian's hope, the one event which will mark the beginning of the completion of God's plan."[1]

The New Testament picture of our Lord's return emphasizes at least six distinct aspects of the time of His coming.

Future. The entire emphasis of the New Testament points to a future return of Christ. He promised "I will come again" (John 14:3). The angels promised He would return (Acts 1:11). The apostles taught the certainty of His future return (Philippians 3:20; Titus 2:13; 2 Peter 3:3-8; 1 John 3:2-3).

Imminent. The return of Jesus Christ is always described as potentially imminent or "at hand" (Revelation 1:3; 22:10). Every generation of believers is warned to be ready for His coming, as Luke 12:40 states: "You also be ready, for the Son of Man is coming at an hour you do not expect" (NKJV). Believers are constantly urged to look for the coming of the Lord (Philippians 3:20; 1 Thessalonians 5:6; Titus 2:13; Hebrews 9:28).

Distant. From God's perspective, Jesus is coming at any moment. But from the human perspective it has already been nearly 2000 years. Jesus hinted at this in the Olivet Discourse in the illustration of the man who traveled into a far country (heaven) and was gone a long time (Matthew 25:14,19). Peter also implies this in his prediction that men will begin to scoff at the second coming after a long period of time (2 Peter 3:3-9).

Undated. The rapture is the next major event on the prophetic calendar, but it is undated, as is the glorious appearing of Christ. Jesus said, "But of that day and hour knoweth no man, no not the angels of heaven" (Matthew 24:36). Later He added, "It is not for you to know the times or the seasons which the Father has put in His own authority" (Acts 1:7 NKJV).

Unexpected. The mass of humanity will not be looking for Christ when He returns (Matthew 24:50). They will be saying "peace and safety" when suddenly caught unprepared by His return. His return will be so unexpected that "as a snare shall it come upon them that dwell on the face of the whole earth" (Luke 21:35).

Sudden. The Bible warns that Jesus will come "as a thief in the night," and "sudden destruction" will come upon the unbelieving world (1 Thessalonians 5:2-3). His return for the bride will occur in a flash, "in a moment, in the twinkling of an eye…for the trumpet shall sound, and the dead [believers] shall be raised incorruptible, and we [living believers] shall be changed" (1 Corinthians 15:52).

The return of Christ is a series of events fulfilling all end-time prophecies. These include predictions of His coming *for* His church and His coming *with* His church. No system of biblical prophecy is adequate without a rapture. The church will be "caught up" and gathered together to the Lord. The only real debate is over the question of when. And *when* the rapture takes place, millions of Christians will disappear in an instant, shaking those left behind and leaving a power vacuum of global proportions that will begin the time of the tribulation.

2

USA OUT—NEW POWER IN

The United States has existed as the world's sole superpower since the dismantling of the Soviet Union at the end of the twentieth century. In the history of the world, no other nation has attained the level of wealth, influence, and power that America has. Yet the occurrence of the rapture—the disappearance of millions, discussed in chapter 1—will transform America's power status overnight, and a new global leadership structure will emerge.

Studies typically reveal that approximately 40 percent of Americans claim to be Christian. At the most conservative end of the spectrum, 10 to 20 percent of Americans hold a biblical view on key Christian beliefs. Using these estimates as a guideline, between 30 and 120 million Americans will instantly disappear if the rapture occurs today! Imagine the numbers of pilots, drivers, homemakers, employees, government and military personnel, teachers, ministers, coaches, business people, and many others who will simply no longer exist on earth.

Surely other nations will be seriously affected as well. But in America, millions and millions of people will suddenly be missing. The rapture will critically destabilize America. It will destabilize the military, the police force, and other organizations that provide social services. The economy itself will be devastated. America will be in trouble, and a new world power will step into the vacuum.

The Post-rapture World Power

In Daniel 9:26, we read that the people who destroyed the

second temple will also provide the leader of the end times. Obviously, the Romans destroyed the second temple. Based on this information, the Bible clearly predicts that the world leader of the future will come from the former Roman Empire.

The Antichrist will not be Chinese or Brazilian or Saudi. He will not be a Muslim or a Jew because the Bible says he does not regard the God of his fathers or any god (Daniel 11:37). He will be either an atheist or a pluralist who believes in himself and ultimately decides, "I am God, and the world should worship me!"

This secular Antichrist from the former Roman Empire will come to power after the rapture. This means I am not looking for the Antichrist today. I am looking for Jesus Christ. I am not even looking for the undertaker. I am looking for the upper-taker—the Lord, who is coming to call us home to be with Him. But once the rapture occurs, the center of world power will shift, and the old Roman Empire—predominantly represented today by the European Union—will suddenly dominate the Western world.

The Leader of the Post-rapture World

What does the Bible predict about this future world leader? Also called "the beast" (Revelation 13:1), a biblical symbol for the Antichrist, he is also referred to as the man of sin, the son of perdition, the wicked one, the lawless one, and the willful king. Again and again, both the Old and the New Testaments tell us that someone is coming who will rule the world. Let's look at 2 Thessalonians 2 to see what Paul has to say about the Antichrist.

His Revelation

Paul says this about the day of the return of Christ to judge the world at the Battle of Armageddon: "Let no man deceive you by any means: for that day shall not come, except there come a falling away first, and that man of sin be revealed, the son of perdition" (2 Thessalonians 2:3).

When Paul says "the man of sin is *revealed*," he uses the Greek word from which we get our word *apocalypse*—the same word used in the title of the book of Revelation. How will he reveal himself? The Antichrist "opposeth and exalteth himself above all that is called God, or that is worshipped; so that he as God sitteth in the temple of God, showing himself that he is God" (2 Thessalonians 2:4).

His Rebellion

After we learn about the revelation of his identity, we read about the rebellion in his heart. He rebels against the God of the Bible, the God of heaven. He rebels against everything that God stands for—the laws of God, the principles of God, the teaching of God. This rebellion causes him to oppose God and exalt himself.

When people do not really believe in the God of the Bible, they end up making a god out of themselves. They become their own god. They decide, "I'm going to run my world by myself. I am going to make all my decisions. I'm going to run my life." A person who is that self-centered and self-focused is the kind of person whom Satan will ultimately indwell and empower to be the final world ruler in the end times. This rebellious Antichrist will sit in the temple of God and insist that he be worshipped as God.

That statement alone tells us that in the last days, when the Antichrist is revealed, there must be a Jewish temple. No Jewish temple exists today. Synagogues abound all over the world, and some of them even include the word *temple* in their name, but they are not the same as the temple referred to in the Bible. The Babylonians and the Romans destroyed the first and second temples long ago.

The temple referred to in this passage is apparently a third temple yet to be built by the Jewish people (see chapter 5). Daniel 9:27 tells us that the Antichrist will eventually betray the nation of Israel by breaking his covenant and treaty with them. He will then enter the rebuilt temple and claim that he is God, demanding that the world worship him as divine.

His Restraint

This one who is revealed, this one who is rebellious, is currently restrained by the power of the Holy Spirit. Paul goes on to say, "And now ye know what withholdeth that he might be revealed in his time" (2 Thessalonians 2:6). Again we see the term referring to the apocalypse, or revelation, of the Antichrist. It cannot happen as long as something is restraining him and holding him back. The very next verse notes, "For the mystery of iniquity doth already work: only he who now letteth will let, until he be taken out of the way" (verse 7).

Notice that the Restrainer is now called "He"—a person. Paul wrote that back in the first century. The "mystery of lawlessness" has been at work ever since. But something, someone, is restraining the revelation of the Antichrist. The only person who qualifies to be a something and yet a He is the Holy Spirit of God. The only person in the whole universe powerful enough to restrain the rise of the Antichrist is God Himself. God, through the person of the Holy Spirit, is restraining the arrival of the Antichrist.

His Resource

Paul goes on to explain that the resource of the Antichrist is Satan himself. He says that once the Restrainer is removed (presumably when the church is raptured home to heaven and the Holy Spirit withdraws His empowerment of the church), the Antichrist will be revealed.

> And then shall that Wicked be revealed, whom the Lord shall consume with the spirit of his mouth, and shall destroy with the brightness of his coming: even him, whose coming is after the working of Satan with all power and signs and lying wonders (2 Thessalonians 2:8-9).

In other words, the power behind the beast is Satan, who is described in the book of Revelation as the dragon. The dragon is one of many powerful symbolic pictures in the book of Revelation. The dragon empowers the beast, and the beast controls the woman who is destined to pervert the world in the last days (Revelation 17–18).

The Spirit of God restrains the Antichrist and keeps him from coming to power even now. That means you and I do not need to be afraid of the Antichrist. I have been in the ministry for 40 years, and I've heard it all. People are always afraid that the latest political leader or tyrant will be the Antichrist. Of course, it never turns out to be that person. Why? Satan cannot empower anybody to be the Antichrist until after the removal of the Restrainer. That has not yet occurred. Once the Restrainer is removed, Satan will indwell this person. Only then will he choose the candidate to be the Antichrist. So that means there is no Antichrist on the scene right now, and there will not be until after the rapture of the church.

However, that does not mean there will not be Antichrist-like individuals. Hitler wanted to exterminate the Jews. Stalin hated Christians and wanted to exterminate them. Today, enemies remain who wish to destroy Jews or Christians. Yet those Antichrist-like attitudes do not mean that those people are the Antichrist. The Bible gives us a very clear picture of this individual and lets us know he can come to power only by the permission of God when the Restrainer is removed.

I hope you understand 2 Thessalonians 2. It is one of the important biblical passages relating to the Antichrist. The Antichrist may be alive somewhere on earth today. He may be moving into power somewhere in the world. He may already *be* in power somewhere in the world. But he cannot be empowered by Satan to function as the Antichrist until after the removal of the Restrainer.

When the Antichrist does come to power, his religion will be one of deception. His resource will be Satan himself. His attitude will be, "The world must follow me, my beliefs, my ideas, and my concepts." John described the Antichrist in Revelation 13:1: "And I stood upon the sand of the sea, and saw a beast rise up out of the sea." John says later the sea is the symbol of humanity. So this beast is a human being—he arises out of humanity.

We are also told in the same verse, "Having seven heads and ten horns, and upon his horns ten crowns, and upon his heads the name of blasphemy." The seven heads and ten horns are identified in the book of Revelation with Satan himself. Then John describes this individual in verse 2 as having the power of a leopard, a bear, and a lion. But the dragon, Satan, is the one who empowers him.

John is using symbolism right out of the book of Daniel in the Old Testament. The symbols of the lion, the bear, and the leopard represent the Gentile world powers that Daniel had predicted would arise in the future. Now John, in the book of Revelation in the New Testament, says the Antichrist is the epitome of all of that. He will serve as the final culmination of the great Gentile world rulers of the last days.

The Antichrist is not a practicing Jew. Why would an orthodox Jew make a treaty with the Jews to protect the Jews? Why would he then break that treaty and turn against his own people? He is not a Muslim. Nothing in the Bible indicates that he is. Everything in Scripture implies the Antichrist is coming from Europe, from the Western world. He will be leading Gentiles.

His Restoration

And then the Scripture says, "And I saw one of his heads as it were wounded to death; and his deadly wound was healed: and all the world wondered after the beast. And they worshipped the dragon which gave power unto the beast" (Revelation 13:3-4). Notice "as it were wounded." It is not clear whether he will literally die, but others will see the Antichrist as one who has come to an end.

Prophecy scholars have long debated this scenario. Is this an attempt to assassinate the Antichrist? Or is this the Antichrist's system that seems to die and then revive? The wound may refer either to the apparent death of the Antichrist himself or to the decline and apparent disappearance of the Roman Empire. The healing of the wound may be either the apparent resurrection of the Antichrist or the revival of the Roman Empire.

In other words, it is not that the Antichrist is assassinated. He does not have multiple heads. It says one of his heads was wounded. He does not have seven heads, one of which is killed. Rather, it sounds as if a part of his system is destroyed. There appears to be destruction, and yet there is a resurrection, if you will, of the Antichrist. Satan cannot resurrect the dead. The idea is used symbolically in the passage. Probably the empire of the Antichrist appears to die out.

If indeed the final empire of Bible prophecy is the Roman Empire, and if the Roman Empire appeared to end yet is revived in the last days, then the reunification of Europe today in the form of the European Union should grab our attention. In 1957, the Treaty of Rome established the European Economic Community, which paved the way for the Single European Act of 1987 and the creation of the European Union. A resurrection is already in process—a revival, a restoration of the kingdom of Antichrist, who will one day emerge out of Europe to rule the world.

His Retaliation

Revelation 11 tells us very clearly that the Antichrist will retaliate against God, the people of God, and the things of God. He will make war on the saints for 42 months—1260 days, or three and a half years. This is not a prophecy about something that happened in the past. This is yet to happen. Revelation 11:2 says the court of the Gentiles and the holy city shall be trod under foot for 42 months. Verse 3 goes on to say, "And I will give power unto my two witnesses, and they shall prophesy a thousand two hundred and threescore days, clothed in sackcloth."

Two Jewish believers will be convinced that Jesus is indeed the Messiah, the Christ. They will prophesy for three and a half years

(42 months). In other words, for the first three and a half years of
the tribulation period, these two witnesses will be preaching to the
people of Israel that Jesus Christ is indeed the promised Messiah
of Israel. As a result, many people will come to faith in Christ (see
chapter 4).

In the meantime, the Bible also makes it clear the Antichrist will
have already risen to power. He will already be ruling over a consol-
idated Roman Empire, or European Union. Revelation 11:5 goes on
to say that the two witnesses will have power to call down fire from
heaven. Verse 6 explains that they will have power to pray so that it
will not rain. Those were miracles Elijah did in the Old Testament.
They will be able to turn water into blood and bring plagues on the
earth. Those were miracles that Moses did in the Old Testament.
These two witnesses come in the spirit and style of Moses and Elijah.

Then verse 7 says, "And when they shall have finished their testimony, the beast that ascendeth out of the bottomless pit shall
make war against them, and shall overcome them, and kill them."
Their dead bodies will lie in the streets of Jerusalem for three and a
half days while the entire world watches them through some kind
of global broadcast. People will send presents to one another and
dance in the streets. They will have a party because the two witnesses are dead.

Then the shock will come. "And after three days and an half the
Spirit of life from God entered into them, and they stood upon
their feet; and great fear fell upon them which saw them" (verse 11).
I would love to be watching CNN or Fox News on that day when
the cameras suddenly zoom in on the dead bodies, and the host says,
"They're getting up! They're alive!" Verse 12 speaks of these two men
then ascending to heaven.

After their disappearance, the Antichrist will pour out his wrath
in retaliation on the nation and people of Israel.

> And they worshipped the dragon which gave power unto
> the beast: and they worshipped the beast, saying, Who is

like unto the beast? Who is able to make war with him?
And there was given unto him a mouth speaking great
things and blasphemies; and power was given unto him
to continue forty and two months (Revelation 13:4-5).

This is the last three and a half years of the seven-year tribulation
period. Next we are told the Antichrist...

opened his mouth in blasphemy against God, to blaspheme his name, and his tabernacle, and them that dwell
in heaven. And it was given unto him to make war with
the saints, and to overcome them: and power was given
him over all kindreds, and tongues, and nations. And
all that dwell upon the earth shall worship him, whose
names are not written in the book of life of the Lamb
slain from the foundation of the world (verses 6-8).

This passage predicts a retaliation of the Antichrist against the
people of Israel—worse than that of the Nazi Holocaust—as Satan
empowers him to try to destroy the earthly people of God. He cannot touch the heavenly people of God who have been taken away
in the rapture of the church. So he will turn his wrath against the
earthly people, the tribulation believers who are coming to faith in
Jesus the Messiah. The Antichrist ultimately will be determined to
conquer the entire world. This will eventually lead to the crisis of
his attack on the nation of Israel, which in turn will lead to the Battle of Armageddon and finally result in his removal and banishment.

His Removal

The Bible powerfully assures us that we don't have to be afraid
of the future. God is in control. God understands what is going to
happen. He sees the future. He knows the future. He controls the
future. Evil exists only by His divine permission. He restrains it. He
will judge it. He will ultimately eliminate it.

Notice the dramatic conclusion in Revelation 19:11-21. Heaven is opened, and a rider comes out on a white horse. He is called Faithful and True. This is Christ Himself, the Word of God, as He is called in verse 13. He judges the nations with a sharp sword—the power of His Word. With a rod of iron, He treads the winepress of the fierceness and wrath of God Almighty. The Battle of Armageddon is over before it begins, for verse 20 says the beast and the false prophet are cast alive into the lake of fire burning with brimstone. Their followers are slain with the sword of His mouth.

Revelation tells us that the victor will be Jesus Christ, not the Antichrist. The power of God, not Satan, will prevail in the end. God's plan for the future is to establish the kingdom of God on earth when the King Himself appears to reign and to rule.

All of these passages remind us that trouble is coming, but they also encourage us that we do not have to be victims of it. When you know Jesus Christ as your personal Savior, your heart and life belong to the King of kings, the Lord of lords, the One who is coming again to reign and rule in righteousness. The rise of the beast will be put down by the power of Christ Himself.

3

WORLD PEACE PROMISED

The third shocking event that will shake the world is a promise of world peace despite world disaster. The book of Revelation tells us clearly that a global economy will arise in the time of the end. Nobody will be able to buy or sell unless he or she has the mark of the beast, the name of the beast, or the number of the beast (Revelation 13:16-18). A world government will dominate the entire planet in the end times, and eventually a world religion as the Antichrist demands that the world worship him as God.

Think of just these first three events. Millions of people are suddenly missing without explanation because of the rapture. The power of world leadership shifts from the United States to Europe. Then a world leader arises and proclaims (despite evidence to the contrary), "Don't be afraid. I can bring peace and stability to the world. What we need is prosperity. What we need is a change of direction. What we need is some hope for the future." That man will be the Antichrist himself.

The Antichrist Comes to Power

Biblical prophecies clearly predict the rise of the Antichrist in the end times. Many people believe those days have already begun. As civilization speeds toward its final destiny, the appearance of a powerful world ruler appears inevitable. A recurring question facing our generation is whether he is already alive and well and moving into power. How can we know who he is? What clues are there to his identity? When will he make his move to control world power and a global economy?

The Bible predicts that worldwide chaos, instability, and disorder will increase as we approach the end of the age. Jesus predicted there would be "wars and rumors of wars…[and] famines and earthquakes in various places" (Matthew 24:6-7). Interestingly, the term *Antichrist* appears only in 1 John 2:18-22; 4:3; and 2 John 7. The apostle John uses it both in the singular ("the antichrist") and in the plural ("many antichrists"). John indicates that his readers have already heard that the Antichrist is coming in the future. Then he surprises them by announcing that many antichrists have already come. He defines these lesser antichrists as liars who deny that Jesus is the Christ (1 John 2:22). In this sense, an antichrist is any false teacher who denies the person and work of Jesus Christ. Such teachers are truly anti (against) Christ.

In 1 John 4:1-3, John warns readers to test the spirits to make sure they are from God. Again, he warns that many false prophets (Greek, *pseudoprophetes*) have "gone out into the world." These are people who don't acknowledge Jesus is from God. In this sense, John announces that the "spirit of antichrist…is already in the world."

Spirit of the Antichrist

In the broadest sense, we can say the spirit of the Antichrist is already at work. This anti-Christian spirit seeks to undermine and reject the truth about Jesus Christ—as it has actively been doing since the first century.

There can be no doubt that the biblical writers believed the spirit of the Antichrist was alive and well in the first century AD. They were not surprised by opposition, persecution, and even execution as they proclaimed their faith in Christ. They were convinced that the spiritual war between Christ and the Antichrist had already begun.

Grant Jeffrey identified numerous examples of early Christian references to the Antichrist in the Apocalypse of Peter, the Didache, the Ascension of Isaiah, and the Pseudo-Titus Epistle, as well as the writings of various church fathers, such as Irenaeus, Jerome, and Hippolytus.[1] Irenaeus, who studied under Polycarp, who in turn was discipled by the apostle John, said the Antichrist shall come as "an apostate," the very embodiment of "satanic apostasy."[2]

From the very beginning of the Christian era, believers were convinced that a world ruler would eventually come on the scene who was the embodiment of Satan. Revelation 12–13 presents an unholy trinity that aligns Satan against the Father, the Antichrist against the Son, and the false prophet against the Holy Spirit. Thus, the real power behind the Antichrist is Satan. The "father of lies" is the perpetrator of the human manifestation of the world's greatest liar and the source of the lie that will condemn multitudes under divine judgment (2 Thessalonians 2:11).

Titles of the Antichrist

The person commonly referred to as the Antichrist is mentioned by many names and titles in Scripture. Each one highlights a facet of his evil character and nature. These word pictures of the Antichrist spark our imaginations to communicate truth. (All the verses in this section are taken from the NIV.)

The beast. "I saw a beast coming out of the sea. It had ten horns and seven heads, with ten crowns on its horns, and on each head a blasphemous name" (Revelation 13:1).

The man of lawlessness. "Don't let anyone deceive you in any way, for that day will not come until the rebellion occurs and the man of lawlessness is revealed, the man doomed to destruction" (2 Thessalonians 2:3).

The lawless one. "And then the lawless one will be revealed, whom the Lord Jesus will overthrow with the breath of his mouth and destroy by the splendor of his coming" (2 Thessalonians 2:8).

The abomination. "So when you see standing in the holy place 'the abomination that causes desolation,' spoken of through the prophet Daniel…" (Matthew 24:15).

The little horn. "While I was thinking about the horns, there before me was another horn, a little one, which came up among them; and three of the first horns were uprooted before it. This horn had eyes like the eyes of a human being and a mouth that spoke boastfully" (Daniel 7:8).

A fierce-looking king. "In the latter part of their reign, when rebels have become completely wicked, a fierce-looking king, a master of intrigue, will arise" (Daniel 8:23).

The ruler who will come. "After the sixty-two 'sevens,' the Anointed One will be put to death and will have nothing. The people of the ruler who will come will destroy the city and the sanctuary" (Daniel 9:26).

The contemptible person. "He will be succeeded by a contemptible person who has not been given the honor of royalty. He will invade the kingdom when its people feel secure, and he will seize it through intrigue" (Daniel 11:21).

The strong-willed king. "The king will do as he pleases. He will exalt and magnify himself above every god and will say unheard-of things against the God of gods. He will be successful until the time of wrath is completed, for what has been determined must take place" (Daniel 11:36).

The worthless shepherd. "For I am going to raise up a shepherd over the land who will not care for the lost, or seek the young, or heal the injured, or feed the healthy, but will eat the meat of the choice sheep, tearing off their hoofs. Woe to the worthless shepherd, who deserts the flock!" (Zechariah 11:16-17).

The Antichrist. "Dear children, this is the last hour; and as you have heard that the antichrist is coming, even now many antichrists have come...Who is the liar? It is whoever denies that Jesus is the Christ. Such a person is the antichrist" (1 John 2:18,22).

Much has been written about the prefix *anti* in connection with the Antichrist. It can mean either "against" (in opposition to) or "instead of" (in place of). Is he the great enemy of Christ and the head of a Gentile world government? If so, then he is most likely to be a Gentile himself. Is he is a false messiah who is accepted by the Jews? In that case, it would stand to reason that he would be Jewish.

Richard Trench writes, "The distinction, then, is plain...*antichristos* [antichrist] denies that there is a Christ; *pseudochristos* [false Christ] affirms himself to be Christ."[3] The biblical picture is that he is both. Initially, he presents himself as the savior of Israel by making a covenant to protect her (Daniel 9:27). In this manner, he appears to be her long-awaited Messiah. But in reality, he is against all that the messianic prophecies foretell about the true Messiah.

His Nationality

Whether the Antichrist is a Jew or a Gentile is not clearly answered in the New Testament. Most prophetic scholars believe he will be a Gentile because...

- He leads the European coalition of Gentile nations (Daniel 7:8-24).

- His covenant with Israel promises Gentile protection for Israel (Daniel 9:27).

- His rule is part of the "time of the Gentiles" and their domination over Israel (Luke 21:24).

These passages make it clear the Antichrist will lead the Western powers, but they do not specifically designate his nationality. It is entirely possible that he could be a European or American who leads the final form of the world government. Daniel 11:37, which says he will not regard the "God of his fathers," can also be translated "gods of his ancestors" (NIV). This makes his background inconclusive. The exegesis of this verse has focused on his atheistic beliefs, regardless of whether he is a Jew or Gentile.[4]

Stephen Miller writes, "This verse states that Antichrist will reject whatever religion is practiced by his ancestors."[5] Charles Feinberg, on the other hand, prefers the reading "God of his fathers," noting that this is the usual expression in the Old Testament for the "God of Abraham, Isaac and Jacob." Feinberg adds, "This is the name of God that is used in the prayer book of the Jews to this very day."[6] Either way, the Antichrist is clearly said to be an unbeliever.

The books of Daniel and Revelation associate the Antichrist with a confederation of ten European nations that correspond in some way to the old Roman Empire. Daniel 2:31-45 symbolizes this by the ten toes of the great statue in Nebuchadnezzar's dream. Daniel 7:19-28 and Revelation 13:1-9 symbolize this by the ten horns on the beast.

In Daniel's prophecies, the Antichrist is always associated with the final phase of the Roman Empire (the fourth kingdom). In Revelation 17:9, he is identified with a city that sits on seven hills (Rome). John uses the symbolic name Babylon, but he clearly indicates he is talking about Rome.

Arno Froese points out that the entire social-political-legal structure of the Western world is essentially European.

> The populations of the USA, Canada and South America are made up mainly of European descendants. Our governments are based on Roman principles…We do well to remember that America, North and South, most of Africa, and Australia are a political reality due to…the greatest power structure ever, Europe.[7]

It is not difficult, given our current international structure and the need for a human leader to guarantee peaceful coexistence, to imagine a powerful world ruler coming on the scene in the immediate future. The spirit of Antichrist is at work today, attempting to lure this world into the lap of Satan. Harvard theologian Harvey Cox warned, "The greatest seducers of history all had one thing in common: they could use the natural needs and instincts of another person for their own selfish ends." He argued that seduction is the most callous form of exploitation because "it tricks the victim into becoming an unwitting accomplice in his own seduction."[8]

The Intellect and Power of the Antichrist

The Antichrist will be the most incredible leader the world has ever known. On the surface he will appear as the epitome of human genius and power. Arthur W. Pink provides this description:

> Satan has had full opportunity afforded him to study fallen human nature…The devil knows full well how to dazzle people by the attraction of power…He knows how to gratify the craving for knowledge…He can delight the ear with music and the eye with entrancing beauty…He knows how to exalt people to dizzy heights of worldly greatness and fame, and how to control that greatness so that it may be employed against God and His people.[9]

Pink lists these characteristics of the Antichrist:

intellectual genius (Daniel 7:20)
oratorical genius (Daniel 7:20)
political genius (Daniel 11:21)
commercial genius (Daniel 8:25)
military genius (Daniel 8:24)
administrative genius (Revelation 13:1-2)
religious genius (2 Thessalonians 2:4)

Perhaps the most telling of his characteristics is depicted in Daniel 11:21, which tells us that he will come to power and "seize the kingdom by intrigue" (NKJV) or "by flatteries" (KJV). Here is a master of deception, empowered by the father of lies.

Grant Jeffrey points out several contrasts between Christ and Antichrist.[10]

CHRIST	ANTICHRIST
the truth	the lie
Holy One	lawless one
man of sorrows	man of sin
Son of God	son of Satan
mystery of godliness	mystery of iniquity
good shepherd	worthless shepherd
exalted on high	cast down to hell
humbled Himself	exalted himself
despised	admired
cleanses the temple	defiles the temple
slain for the people	slays the people
the Lamb	the beast

A simple survey of the traits of the Antichrist confirms the idea that he is both a false Christ (*pseudochristos*) and an enemy of Christ (*antichristos*). He masquerades as an angel of light only to plunge the world into spiritual darkness. Like Satan, he is a destroyer rather than a builder. In every thinkable way, he will operate just like Satan, who will indwell and empower him.

The Restless Search

Many believe the Antichrist is alive and well today. Yet as we have seen, the Antichrist will not come to power until after the rapture. Any apparent delay is not due to God's indecision but to the fact that He has not let us in on the secret. Nor has He revealed this to Satan, who is a limited, finite being. Satan himself is left guessing when the rapture might occur. This means he must have a man in mind to indwell as the Antichrist in every generation. In other words, any one of a number of people could have been the Antichrist, but only one will be. Satan too must keep selecting candidates and waiting for God's timing.

The apostle Paul comments on this in 2 Thessalonians 2:1-12, when he tells us, "that day will not come until the rebellion occurs and the man of lawlessness is revealed" (verse 3 NIV). Next, he tells us that "you know what is holding him back, so that he may be revealed at the proper time" (verse 6 NIV). Only after the rapture of the church will the identity of the Antichrist be revealed. In other words, you don't want to know who he is. If you ever do figure out who he is, you have been left behind!

Satan must prepare a man to be his crowning achievement in every generation, so it should not surprise us that several candidates have appeared in human history only to vanish away. Satan must wait on God's timing, so he is defeated before he even begins his final assault on God. He can't make his move until God removes the restraining power of the Holy Spirit indwelling the church. Therefore, the Spirit is the agent and the church is the means by which God restrains Satan's diabolical plan until the Father calls us home to heaven.

Satan's doom is already assured, but the battle is far from over. He still "prowls around like a roaring lion looking for someone to devour" (1 Peter 5:8 NIV). He has fallen from heaven (Isaiah 14:12). He was condemned in Eden (Genesis 3:14). He accuses the believers (Revelation 12:10). Eventually, he will be cast out of heaven permanently and will expend his wrath on the earth (Revelation 12:7-12). He will be defeated at Armageddon and cast into the abyss for 1000 years (Revelation 19:11–20:3). Finally he will be thrown into the lake of fire, where he will remain forever (Revelation 20:10).

In the meantime, Satan waits for his opportunity to destroy the whole world and the ultimate plan of God. He may be a defeated foe, but he has every intention of keeping up the fight to the very end. Even now he is moving about restlessly, searching for the right man to be the Antichrist.

Ten Keys to the Identity of the Antichrist

The Bible offers at least ten keys to identifying the Antichrist when he does come to power. They provide enough details to give a general idea of who he will be when Satan inspires him to make his move onto the world scene. These clues also make it clear that only one person in history will fit this description. There have been many prototypes, but there will only be one Antichrist. (The following verses are from the NKJV.)

He will rise to power in the last days. "I am making known to you what shall happen in the latter time of the indignation; for at the appointed time the end shall be…A king shall arise, having fierce features, who understands sinister schemes" (Daniel 8:19,23).

He will rule the whole world. "It was granted to him to make war with the saints and to overcome them. And authority was given him over every tribe, tongue, and nation" (Revelation 13:7).

His headquarters will be in Rome. "The beast that you saw was, and is not, and will ascend out of the bottomless pit and go to perdition. And those who dwell on the earth will marvel, whose names are not written in the Book of Life from the foundation of the world, when they see the beast that was, and is not, and yet is. Here is the mind which has wisdom: The seven heads are seven mountains on which the woman sits" (Revelation 17:8-9).

He is intelligent and persuasive. "…the ten horns that were on its head, and the other horn which came up, before which three fell, namely, that horn which had eyes and a mouth which spoke pompous words, whose appearance was greater than his fellows" (Daniel 7:20).

He rules by international consent. "The ten horns which you saw are ten kings who have received no kingdom as yet, but they receive authority for one hour as kings with the beast. These are of one mind, and they will give their power and authority to the beast" (Revelation 17:12-13).

He rules by deception. "His power shall be mighty, but not by his own power; he shall destroy fearfully, and shall prosper and thrive; he shall destroy the mighty, and also the holy people. Through his cunning he shall cause deceit to prosper under his rule; and he shall exalt himself in his heart. He shall destroy many in their prosperity. He shall even rise against the Prince of princes; but he shall be broken without human means" (Daniel 8:24-25).

He controls the global economy. "He causes all, both small and great, rich and poor, free and slave, to receive a mark on their right hand or on their foreheads, and that no one may buy or sell except one who has the mark or the name of the beast, or the number of his name" (Revelation 13:16-17).

He will make a peace treaty with Israel. "Then he shall confirm a covenant with many for one week; but in the middle of the week he shall bring an end to sacrifice and offering. And on the wing of abominations shall be one who makes desolate, even until the consummation, which is determined, is poured out on the desolate" (Daniel 9:27).

He will break the treaty and invade Israel. "And after the sixty-two weeks Messiah shall be cut off, but not for Himself; and the people of the prince who is to come shall destroy the city and the sanctuary. The end of it shall be with a flood, and till the end of the war desolations are determined" (Daniel 9:26).

He will claim to be God. "…who opposes and exalts himself above all that is called God or that is worshiped, so that he sits as God in the temple of God, showing himself that he is God" (2 Thessalonians 2:4).

The Bible gives many other details regarding the Antichrist. But the general picture is that of a person who rises to power over the Western world. Whether he is Jewish or Gentile is not entirely clear. What is clear, however, is that he will control the last great source of Gentile world power. From his base in the West, he will extend his control over the entire world. For all practical purposes, he will administrate the world government and the global economy, assisted by the leader of the world religion (Revelation 13:11-18). He may be moving into power at this very moment, but only time will reveal his true identity.

When he does come to power, the Antichrist will apparently promise to ensure world peace through a series of international alliances, treaties, and agreements (Daniel 8:24; Revelation 17:12). Despite his promises of peace, his international policies will inevitably plunge the world into the greatest war of all time.

The False Prophet Prepares the Way

Despite the popular discussions about the future Antichrist, he will not come to power alone. His success will result from a world-wide spiritual deception perpetrated by the false prophet. Using miraculous signs, the false prophet will convince the public that the Antichrist is the leader they have been seeking. The ultimate deception of the end times will involve the worldwide worship of the Antichrist. This will be encouraged by the false prophet (Revelation 19:20; 20:10), whom John describes as the second beast (Revelation 13:11-17). Like the Antichrist, his identity is not clearly revealed, but several clues are given to help us know who he is.

J. Dwight Pentecost observes that the false prophet serves as the spokesperson for the Antichrist. He states that the spirit of Antichrist "will culminate in the Beasts in their corporate ministries... The first Beast will be in direct opposition to Christ...and the second Beast will assume the place of leadership in the religious realm which rightly belongs to Christ."[11]

Revelation 13 presents ten identifying features of the false prophet. He...

> rises out of the earth (verse 11)
> controls religious affairs (verse 11)
> is motivated by Satan (verse 11)
> promotes the worship of the beast (verse 12)

performs signs and miracles (verse 13)
deceives the whole world (verse 14)
empowers the image of the beast (verse 15)
kills all who refuse to worship (verse 15)
controls all economic commerce (verse 17)
controls the mark of the beast (verses 17-18)

Biblical scholars are divided on the matter of the identity of the false prophet. Some believe that he will be Jewish, while others believe he will be a Gentile. The biblical record itself is inconclusive. However, when we observe the relationship of the false prophet to the great prostitute (Revelation 17), we immediately notice his connection to the city on seven hills (verses 7,9) that rules "over the kings of the earth" (verse 18). John's description of Babylon clearly refers to Rome.

Little has been written about the false prophet compared to the volumes of material about the Antichrist.[12] Thomas Ice and Timothy Demy describe the relationship between the two.

> The Antichrist and the false prophet are two separate individuals who will work toward a common, deceptive goal. Their roles and relationship will be that which was common in the ancient world between a ruler (Antichrist) and the high priest (False Prophet) of the national religion.[13]

The false prophet is depicted in the Revelation as one who uses miraculous signs and wonders to deceive the world into worshipping the Antichrist. Ice and Demy remark, "Even though this is yet a future event, the lesson to be learned for our own day is that one must exercise discernment, especially in the area of religion—even when miracles appear to vindicate the messenger."[14]

A century ago, Samuel Andrews argued that the work of the false prophet will be to extend his ecclesiastical administration over the whole earth by establishing the church of the Antichrist as the counterfeit of the true church.[15] In other words, the false prophet will focus on corrupting Christianity rather than denying it. Only in this way could the Antichrist sit in the temple of God, demanding to be worshipped as God (see Isaiah 14:12-14).

Remember, in Satan's temptation of Christ, his goal was to receive worship (Matthew 4:8-10). In fact, Satan offered to surrender the entire world to Christ if He would worship him. It should not surprise us that the goal of the Satan-inspired false prophet will be to get the whole world to bow down to the Antichrist, who is the personification of Satan himself.

Together, Satan (the dragon), the Antichrist (the beast of sea), and the false prophet (the beast of earth) comprise an unholy trinity that is a counterfeit of the triune God. Satan opposes the Father, the Antichrist opposes the Son, and the false prophet opposes the Holy Spirit. Satan will use this ungodly alliance in his final attempt to overthrow the work of God on the earth.

The method of their diabolical attempt is explained in the biblical record. The Antichrist dare not appear until after the "rebellion" (2 Thessalonians 2:3 NIV) or "falling away" (KJV) of apostasy. In the meantime, the spirit of the Antichrist (lawlessness) is already at work, attempting to pervert the gospel and to corrupt the true church. When this process is sufficiently established, the false prophet will arise to prepare for the coming of the Antichrist. To accomplish the final deception, he will have to control the entire world.

4

TWO DEAD MEN AND A NATION COME TO LIFE

How would you react if you saw not one man, but two men return to life after being dead three days? You would likely be skeptical. But what if the event was caught on live video and rebroadcast worldwide for everyone to see?

This double resurrection is the fourth shocking event that will shake the world. Two dead men will suddenly come back to life. In Revelation 11, we find the prophecy of the two witnesses who will come on the scene in the last days—after the rapture, during the tribulation.

When the Antichrist rises to power after the rapture of the church, he will try to control the world by imposing global economic control. It will affect virtually every person in the world. Eventually he will also deceive the world into thinking he is God.

During this time, a new Jewish temple will be completed in Jerusalem. In Revelation 11:1-2, the apostle John measured the temple and was told it will be trampled for 42 months. We will address this topic in greater detail later, but it is important to note that the temple will be completed in the first half of the seven-year tribulation. At the midpoint of the tribulation, the Antichrist will defile the temple and declare himself to be God.

Introducing the Two Witnesses

Scripture indicates that in the meantime, God will raise up from the Jewish people two witnesses who will proclaim the truth—that

Christ is the Messiah, that the rapture has occurred, and that the unsaved world has been left behind. "And I will give power unto my two witnesses, and they shall prophesy a thousand two hundred and threescore days, clothed in sackcloth" (Revelation 11:3).

The 1260 days are the three and a half years of the tribulation period, or 42 months. Those terms are used repeatedly in the book of Revelation to remind us that the ministry of the two witnesses begins shortly after the rapture occurs. God will move on the hearts of two significant Jewish leaders who know enough about the New Testament to realize, "My goodness, the rapture has occurred. The church is gone. We've been left behind. We need to preach the truth to our people." Revelation notes that God will use them powerfully. They will proclaim the message. Scripture says they will have the power to shut up heaven so it will not rain and to call down fire from heaven, even as Elijah did in the Old Testament. And they will have power to turn water into blood, as Moses did (Revelation 11:5-6).

They are not necessarily Moses and Elijah literally, but they will come in the spirit of Moses and Elijah, just as John the Baptist did (Matthew 17:10-13). On the day of Jesus's transfiguration on the mountain in front of three disciples, two men appeared with Him—Moses and Elijah (Matthew 17:3). They represented the Law and the prophets, as if to say, "The message of the Law and the message of the prophets affirm the fact that Jesus is indeed the Messiah." The example of these witnesses already holds biblical precedence.

The Activities of the Two Witnesses

Their ministry is characterized in conduct by four great miraculous powers. They can...

> kill their enemies with fire
> withhold rain for three and a half years
> turn water into blood
> bring plagues on the earth
>   (Exodus 7–11; 1 Kings 17:1; 2 Kings 1:10-15)

Why these specific miracles? First, the two witnesses will use them to defend themselves until their ministry is over (Revelation 11:5). But second, these specific miracles occur because of their significance to Israel. They will be used to turn the hearts of the Jews to the Lord in preparation for the coming King.[1]

The Death of the Two Witnesses

> When they shall have finished their testimony, the beast that ascendeth out of the bottomless pit shall make war against them, and shall overcome them, and kill them. And their dead bodies shall lie in the street of the great city, which spiritually is called Sodom and Egypt, where also our Lord was crucified (Revelation 11:7-8).

The two witnesses will preach in Jerusalem in the last days during the first three and a half years of the tribulation period. Then suddenly they are killed, executed by the Antichrist—the beast. Scripture says their bodies will lie in the street for three and a half days. The Antichrist will not allow them to be buried.

The Resurrection and Rapture of the Two Witnesses

Suddenly, a stunning shock:

> And after three days and an half the Spirit of life from God entered into them, and they stood upon their feet; and great fear fell upon them which saw them. And they heard a great voice from heaven saying unto them, Come up hither. And they ascended up to heaven (Revelation 11:11-12).

A mini-rapture occurs with the two witnesses. Why would God empower them to preach, allow them to be executed, and then raise them from the dead and rapture them to heaven? To demonstrate to the world one last time, before the end finally comes, that the resurrection is real and the rapture is true. Two dead men come to life to say to the world, "The message of the Word of God indeed is true."

The Aftermath of the Two Witnesses

In 2010 an epic magnitude 7 earthquake rocked the island nation of Haiti. Death-toll estimates range from 100,000 to more than 200,000, and thousands more were injured. The world responded with an outpouring of assistance. The aftermath of the two witnesses ascending to heaven will include a similar devastation—this time in the city of Jerusalem.

Revelation 11:13 describes a dramatic devastation of Jerusalem immediately following the ascension of these two witnesses: "In the same hour there was a great earthquake, and a tenth of the city fell. In the earthquake seven thousand people were killed, and the rest were afraid and gave glory to the God of heaven" (NKJV). An amazing 10 percent of the city will fall in a massive earthquake that will kill 7000 people. The result will be one of fear among the people of Jerusalem. The recognition that "the rest were afraid and gave glory to the God of heaven" indicates that those remaining at least recognized God was at work. Perhaps many Jews will come to faith in Christ as a result of this event, which will take place at the midpoint of the seven-year tribulation period.

How will many Jews come to faith in Jesus as Messiah during this time of tribulation? The conversion of the Jewish people is clearly predicted in the Bible, both in the Old Testament and in the New Testament. The principle comes right out of the experience of the apostle Paul himself. Remember, Jesus was Jewish, all the disciples were Jewish, and the apostle Paul was Jewish. Yet on the road to Damascus, Paul met Jesus, the Christ, the Messiah, the Savior, and had a personal encounter with Him. And Paul, quoting the Old Testament, said, "For whosoever shall call upon the name of the Lord shall be saved" (Romans 10:13).

Then Paul predicted that all Israel will ultimately be saved (Romans 11:26). The idea of the total family of God—the Old Testament people of God and the New Testament people of God—coming into a personal relationship with Him is clearly taught throughout the Bible. Early church fathers, such as Irenaeus and Justin Martyr, believed this. The early Reformers wrote and taught often about the future conversion of the Jews. The Puritans wrote about it in many of their messages and sermons as they understood that the Bible was predicting the conversion of the Jewish people.

This is not an anti-Jewish concept at all. In fact, it is a very pro-God concept—God wants to bring all of His people into a relationship with Himself. God is "not willing that any should perish, but that all should come to repentance" (2 Peter 3:9). All people, both Jews and Gentiles, are called to come to faith and to an experience with the Lord Himself.

The Prophecy of Ezekiel

The Hebrew Scriptures have much to say about the coming of the future Savior, Messiah, King, and Ruler. Consider this example from the prophet Ezekiel.

> And David my servant shall be king over them; and they all shall have one shepherd: they shall also walk in my judgments, and observe my statutes, and do them. And they shall dwell in the land that I have given unto Jacob my servant, wherein your fathers have dwelt; and they shall dwell therein, even they, and their children, and their children's children for ever: and my servant David shall be their prince for ever (Ezekiel 37:24-25).

When Ezekiel wrote this, David had been dead for 500 years. Yet Ezekiel the prophet was saying that a time is coming when the nation and people of Israel will go back to the land, and David will rule over them.

Some take this as David being literally resurrected to rule over Israel in the messianic kingdom. Others suggest it is the greater Son of David—Jesus Christ Himself, the Son of Abraham, the Son of David, who will reign and rule in David's place and fulfill the promise of the Old Testament. Either way, the line of David will never be removed from the throne of Israel, and the kingdom of God will ultimately become a reality on earth.

This much is obvious—whoever this is will rule forever. He must be an eternal individual, eternally alive. He is the eternal Son of God. "Moreover I will make a covenant of peace with them; it shall be an everlasting covenant with them: and I will place them, and multiply them, and will set my sanctuary in the midst of them for evermore" (Ezekiel 37:26).

This did not happen in ancient history. The Jewish people were scattered by the Babylonians in 586 BC. They returned to the land, only to be scattered by the Romans in AD 70. They had been mostly missing from the Promised Land for almost 1900 years when they finally returned in the twentieth century.

God promised He would one day bring His people back to the land so He could ultimately bring them back to Himself. Paul announces this in the New Testament. Remember, Paul's Jewish name was Saul. On the road to Damascus, he had an encounter with Christ. He believed that Jesus is the Messiah, the Son of God. He committed his heart and life to Him, and then he became an apostle, preaching the gospel to both the Jews and the Gentiles, calling both groups to faith in Christ.

Think of how incredible that would have been at that time. When Paul launched his missionary campaign to the Gentiles, there were hardly any Gentile believers. Paul was reaching out beyond his comfort zone, beyond his own cultural boundaries, and recognizing that the promise of the Messiah is for both the Jew and the Gentile. God is calling all men everywhere to repent and to come to faith in the Son of God, who died on the cross for their sins. Paul tells us in the book of Romans that according to the election of grace, only a few of the Jewish people will respond. But a final repentance is coming for the nation and people of God. Ultimately, one day, all Israel will be saved (Romans 11:26).

What will it take for that to happen? What will it take for the Jewish people to finally come to the realization that the Messiah they are looking for is not coming in the future—He has already come in the past and will come again to set up His kingdom on earth? What will it take to ultimately bring them to real faith?

Perhaps you have intellectually struggled, wondering whether the Bible really says anything about the future of the people and nation of Israel. What can you expect as a Jewish person? What can you expect as a Gentile? The Jewish prophets in the Old Testament foresaw a time of spiritual transformation that would come to the people of Israel, a time of heart conversion to the Lord Himself. Yet in predicting that, they also foresaw a time of trouble as well.

Ezekiel 38–39 tells us that a war involving Israel is coming in the Middle East. This conflict has come to be known as the Battle of Gog and Magog. Gog is the leader of the people of Magog, and he will attack the nation and people of Israel.

> Son of man, set thy face against Gog, the land of Magog, the chief prince of Meshech and Tubal, and prophesy against him, and say, Thus saith the Lord GOD; Behold, I am against thee, O Gog, the chief prince of Meshech and Tubal: and I will turn thee back, and put hooks into thy jaws, and I will bring thee forth, and all thine army, horses and horsemen, all of them clothed with all sorts of armor, even a great company with bucklers and shields, all of them handling swords (Ezekiel 38:2-4).

We are told this conflict takes place on the mountains of Israel. Then Ezekiel names the alliance that will come with Gog:

• Persia, the ancient name of Iran

- Cush, the ancient name of Sudan and that part of Africa that today is under Islamic control

- Libya, in North Africa

- Gomer and Togarmah, ancient terms for Turkey, "and many people with thee"

How will this happen? This passage prophesies an invasion of Israel by an alliance of what are today the Muslim-led nations around it, led by Magog, whom many agree is Russia (or at least part of it). When will this occur?

> After many days thou shalt be visited: in the latter years thou shalt come into the land that is brought back from the sword, and is gathered out of many people, against the mountains of Israel…And thou shalt say, I will go up to the land of unwalled villages; I will go to them that are at rest, that dwell safely, all of them dwelling without walls, and having neither bars nor gates (Ezekiel 38:8,11).

In other words, Ezekiel prophesied that Israel would someday return to the land. We have already seen that promise fulfilled. They will dwell in relative peace, in safety and stability. In the modern world, walled villages are rather inconsequential, if only because of the threat of missiles and bombs. The cities of Israel today spill out over the ancient walls into the territories God had promised to them.

In effect, God was saying, "I will be with My people. I will bless My people. They will return to the land. But once they have returned, this invasion will occur in the future." An Old Testament Jewish prophet predicted that, and he said that all of these nations will form an alliance against Israel. That has never happened. The Jews today fully understand that the battle of Gog and Magog is yet to come. This is not something that happened in the past. "And it shall come to pass," the Lord says (Ezekiel 38:18). God is saying, "This is what I have determined."

When will it happen? Verse 12 says it will happen when Israel is "gathered out of the nations." When this invasion occurs, some nations will object. Among them, in verse 13, are "Sheba, and Dedan," cities that are today in Saudi Arabia. "The merchants of Tarshish" is a reference to Europe. And "the young lions thereof" may be a veiled reference to America's connection to Europe (possibly referring to all the distant nations, including the Americas and Australia). Europe and Saudi Arabia will object, but they will not do anything about it. They will not intervene. Instead, Ezekiel says in verse 15, the invasion will come "out of the north parts." "Thou shalt come up against my people of Israel…in the latter days," verse 16 says. In fact, when it happens, God asks rhetorically, "Art thou he of whom I have spoken in old time by my servants the prophets of Israel, which prophesied in those days many years that I would bring thee against them?" (verse 17).

A Middle East crisis is coming—an invasion of the land and people of Israel, which the people of Israel today greatly fear. And yet the Bible says God will intervene. God will defend them and defeat the enemy. That has never happened. This is yet to happen. In the future, God will intervene, the armies of Gog and Magog will be destroyed, and the Lord God will reveal Himself in power and in glory.

Ezekiel 39:22 teaches, "So the house of Israel shall know that I am the LORD their God from that day and forward." Notice that in the English Bible the word "LORD" is full capitalization. This denotes the Hebrew term *Yahweh*, the personal name of God. God says from that point on that the people will know He is the Lord their God. When will this happen? Verse 25 says it will happen when God will "bring again the captivity of Jacob, and have mercy upon the whole house of Israel." The battle of Gog and Magog will be the beginning of Israel's returning to the Lord. But her final and full conversion to Christ will come during or near the end of the tribulation. The events related to the two witnesses halfway through the tribulation will serve as a further witness that will draw the Jewish people to faith in Jesus as the Messiah.

Promise of Zephaniah

We have seen that the prophet indicated that in the last days, Israel would come back into the land in unbelief. When the invasion of Ezekiel 38–39 occurs, Israel will call on the Lord, and He will intervene. When they turn to the One whom they pierced, Zechariah says, and mourn for Him and call upon Him, they will be saved (Zechariah 12:10; 13:1). Other prophets foresaw this as well. Here's one example.

> Gather yourselves together, yea, gather together, O nation not desired; before the decree bring forth, before the day pass as the chaff, before the fierce anger of the LORD come upon you, before the day of the LORD's anger come upon you. Seek ye the LORD, all ye meek of the earth, which have wrought his judgment; seek righteousness, seek meekness: it may be ye shall be hid in the day of the LORD's anger (Zephaniah 2:1-3).

Zephaniah repeatedly entreats his people to turn to the Lord and be changed before the judgment of God falls. He assures them that God will come and will change them, deliver them, and spare them before the great day of His wrath. This will take place during the tribulation. God's people, the Jews, will respond to the judgments and activities of this time by turning to Jesus as the Messiah.

The Apostle Paul's Prediction

How powerfully did that prediction impact the heart and life of Paul? If anybody loved the Jewish people and cared about their spiritual well-being, it was certainly the apostle Paul, who had been a rabbi and Pharisee who was committed to the principles of the Old Testament. He had been looking for the coming of the Messiah. He became convinced on the road to Damascus that Jesus of Nazareth was that Messiah, the promised Savior.

In Acts 9, we have the powerful story of Paul's own conversion. When he cried out, "Who are You, Lord?" the voice responded, "I am Jesus, whom you are persecuting." And Paul said, "Lord, what do You want me to do?" (Acts 9:5-6 NKJV).

Paul's life was changed. His soul was converted, his heart was transformed, and his mission was changed. He spent the rest of his life preaching to both Jews and Gentiles that Jesus Christ is indeed the Savior, the Messiah, who died for their sins on the cross and rose from the dead. Paul preached that Jews and Gentiles could know the risen Lord themselves by faith in Him.

This same apostle wrote the New Testament letter to the church in Rome. In Romans 10–11, he poured out his heart, soul, and concern about the nation and people of Israel.

> Brethren, my heart's desire and prayer to God for Israel is, that they might be saved. For I bear them record that they have a zeal of God, but not according to knowledge. For they being ignorant of God's righteousness, and going about to establish their own righteousness, have not submitted themselves unto the righteousness of God (Romans 10:1-3).

If you are of Jewish background, please be assured that Paul is simply saying, "Your attempt to follow the commandments and the Law and to establish your own personal righteousness will eventually exhaust you. Every human being (Jew and Gentile) fails and falls short of God's standards. The righteousness of God is available only by faith." As verse 4 notes, "For Christ is the end of the law for righteousness to every one that believeth."

Then Paul quotes passage after passage from the Hebrew Scriptures, showing that God's love and grace are shown through His Son, who came to die for the sins of mankind and calls us to faith in Him.

Finally Paul says in Romans 11:25-26 that one day, all the house of Israel will be saved. In the meantime, he makes it clear—"whosoever shall call upon the name of the Lord shall be saved" (Romans 10:13).

This applies to anybody, anywhere, Jew or Gentile, every person—it does not matter who you are. Jesus Christ, the Savior, died for your sins. If you put your faith and trust in Him and call on the name of the Lord, you will be saved. But then Paul says, "Only a remnant among my own people are coming to faith in the Messiah. It breaks my heart because I know what's going to happen in the future."

In the future, trouble, chaos, and judgment will come. Paul had read about all that in the Old Testament prophecies we have seen. Those passages, he realized, revealed that Israel won't cry out to the Messiah—the One whom they have pierced—until the people are gathered back to the land the second time and they are facing extinction in what the Old Testament calls "the time of Jacob's trouble" (Jeremiah 30:7). And so he says, "Blindness in part is happened to Israel, until the fulness of the Gentiles be come in" (Romans 11:25).

God is giving the Gentiles an opportunity to be saved. Ultimately, "all Israel shall be saved: as it is written, There shall come out of Zion the Deliverer, and shall turn away ungodliness from Jacob" (verse 26). Paul was quoting the Old Testament. In other words, in the last days, finally, all Israel will be saved. This does not mean that every Jewish person who has ever lived will be saved, just as not every Gentile person who has ever lived will be saved. Rather, it means that at the end of time, the nation and people of Israel will finally turn to the Messiah.

But Paul's desire was that people should turn to Him now, before that time comes. Come to Him now while there is hope for your destiny. God loved us so much that He sent His Son into the world, not just to teach us how to be better people, but to go to the cross and die for our sins. Only the blood of the Son of God could atone for our sins. Only the blood of a perfect sacrifice was sufficient to pay for sin. We are far from perfect, so we could never be good enough to earn a relationship with God.

Many Jewish people miss the truth today, but it will become clear after the rapture. Two witnesses will serve as tremendous evangelists of their fellow Jews, resulting in many giving glory to God.

5

THE DOME OF THE
ROCK DESTROYED

The fifth shocking event that will shake the world will be the construction of a third Jewish temple, which will probably mean that the Dome of the Rock will be destroyed. Second Thessalonians 2:3-4 tells us that the Antichrist, the man of sin, the son of perdition, the world ruler, will go to this new temple of God, claiming that he is God and demanding that the world worship him as God. The Antichrist's ultimate goal is not only to control the world but also to insist that the world worship him as if he were God.

If he is going to do that in the temple of God, then the temple has to be a Jewish temple. The original Jewish temples were built on the Temple Mount, where the Dome of the Rock sits today. The first temple, built by Solomon in 964 BC, was destroyed by the Babylonians in 586 BC. The second temple, built by Zerubbabel in 515 BC and later expanded by King Herod, was destroyed by the Romans in AD 70.

The passage in 2 Thessalonians implies that there will one day be a third temple. I don't know how or when that will happen. The temple could be rebuilt either before or after the rapture. It could be a concession for the peace process in the Middle East, or the Dome of the Rock could be destroyed in an act of war or terrorism or by an earthquake. But we do know that the temple will be rebuilt, as Dr. Tim LaHaye explains.

Several passages of Scripture refer to the Temple of the end time. In Matthew 24:15 the Lord Jesus referred to the "abomination that causes desolation, spoken of through the prophet Daniel," indicating that at the end time, in the middle of the tribulation period as Daniel predicted, a temple will be desecrated by the Antichrist. In order for this to be fulfilled it must first be rebuilt. Likewise, in 2 Thessalonians 2:1-13 the Apostle Paul predicted that the Antichrist, in the middle of the tribulation, would defy God by sitting in the Temple of God and presenting himself to the world as God. In order for him to do this that temple has to be rebuilt.[1]

Nearly 2000 years have passed since a Jewish temple sat on Mount Moriah. A Muslim shrine, the Dome of the Rock, has stood on the site of the ancient Jewish temple since AD 691. Talk of building a third temple has circulated since the Jewish people began returning to the Promised Land. Presently, the Temple Institute in Jerusalem is dedicated to reconstructing the instruments of worship for the new temple. However, the new temple is not likely to be built on Mount Moriah as long as the Dome of the Rock stands there.

When and Where Will the New Temple Be Built?

When will the new Jewish temple be built, and how will this be accomplished on the Temple Mount? The people of Israel are anxious to rebuild a new temple, and many preparations have been made to that end already. Priests' vestments and vessels to be used in temple services have been prepared, and priests are being trained. The main hindrance is the building site itself. The Temple Mount is home not only to the Dome of the Rock but also another Islamic holy place, the Al-Aqsa Mosque.

Can the temple be constructed next to or in place of these Islamic shrines? That depends on a determination of where the previous Jewish temples stood. Archaeological findings have led to three main theories regarding the location of the previous temple, destroyed by the Romans in AD 70.[2]

First, Tel Aviv architect Tuvia Sagiv claims that the temple was at the southwestern corner of the Temple Mount, near where the Al-Aqsa Mosque is today. He suggests radar and thermographic scans give evidence of vaults underground, such as would be expected beneath the temple.

Second, former Hebrew University physicist Asher Kaufman believes the temple was built at the northwestern corner of the Temple Mount, about 330 feet from the present Dome of the Rock. He bases this on an ancient artifact found at the site, believed to be the foundation stone of the Holy of Holies.

Some suggest this is revealed in Scripture as well. In Revelation 11:1, the apostle John was told to measure the temple and the altar. But in verse 2, the angel instructed him not to include the Court of the Gentiles: "But the court which is without the temple leave out, and measure it not; for it is given unto the Gentiles: and the holy city shall they tread under foot forty and two months."

In this vision, the rebuilt Court of the Gentiles will still be under Gentile (non-Jewish) control. Some believe this prophecy implies that the Dome of the Rock and Jewish temple will coexist in the future.

Yet there is also a third, more commonly held view. Several archaeologists believe the temple stood exactly where the Dome of the Rock is today. This is based on existing remains found on the Temple Mount as well as clues in its eastern wall. It is also derived from the belief that the arrangement of the temple courts would be in the central part of the Mount.

The conclusion to this dilemma will obviously have to await further excavations, which in turn are hampered by the political situation in the area. Islamic excavations have endeavored to destroy evidence of the presence of past Jewish temples on the Temple Mount. Israeli excavations have been severely limited by Muslims, who have control of the holy sites on the Mount. Israel made that concession following the Israeli conquest of Jerusalem in the Six-Day War of 1967.

But what preparations exist for this future Jewish temple? As we have seen, after the rapture and halfway through the seven-year tribulation, the Antichrist will desecrate the temple. Therefore, the temple must be completed and in use by that time. If the rapture took place today, could a rebuilt temple and renewed sacrificial system be completed in three and a half years?

A look at the temple preparations, the temple tools, the reformed Sanhedrin, and the mysterious Ark of the Covenant reveal that such change could quickly take place.

Temple Preparations

Much misinformation can be found regarding the current state of temple preparations, but the planning is clearly underway. In 2013, the Temple Institute publicly unveiled…

> complete and highly detailed blueprints of the Sanhedrin Assembly Hall, the Chamber of Hewn Stone, part of the Holy Temple complex itself. These plans, drawn up by a top Israeli architectural firm hired by the Temple Institute, incorporate modern technological innovation while remaining true to the specific requirements of the Sanhedrin. These plans represent the first stage in the drawing up of comprehensive architectural plans for the entire Holy Temple complex.[3]

In addition to the work of the Temple Institute, planning has been in the works for some time among a wide variety of groups.

> In November 1990 a small group of Israeli government representatives, architects, engineers, rabbis, lawyers, and archaeologists met to discuss solutions to the practical problems in rebuilding the Temple. They estimated it would take one to two years to build the basic Temple

structure. Naturally, the final decorations and finishing details would take ten to twenty years, as it did with the Second Temple.[4]

In today's technological world, a nuclear power plant can be built in three years. The Jewish people certainly have the time, ability, and motivation to quickly construct a new temple when the opportunity arises.

Temple Tools

In the book *Israel Under Fire*, John Ankerberg and Jimmy De-Young interview one of the current Jewish priests affiliated with the Temple Institute and its progress.[5] They note that the following temple tools have already been prepared.

The high priestly crown. The authors note that the crown for the high priest is made out of 24-karat gold. It is designed to fit the head of the one designated by the Sanhedrin as the high priest. This is performed by attaching a blue cord to the open-ended crown. Twenty-four-karat gold is used because of its softness. The crown must be pliable enough to form to the headdress of the high priest.

The menorah. There has been some speculation that the original menorah (the traditional Jewish candle stand) from the first Jewish temple rests in the basement of the Vatican in Rome. According to legend, General Titus and the Roman army carried it back to Rome after destroying the second temple in AD 70. In Rome, a relief on the Arch of Titus indicates the menorah was included in the implements taken by the Romans during the war.

In 1996, the Israeli government dispatched the Minister of Religious Affairs to Rome to ask the pope to either confirm or deny the Vatican's possession of the menorah. The pope would neither confirm nor deny, leaving this mystery open to further speculation. Regardless, the Temple Institute has designed its own menorah for use in the next temple. It is currently on display for public viewing in Israel. This replica of the original contains 90 pounds of gold.

The table of showbread. The Temple Institute also claims to have designed the table of showbread mentioned in temple worship. They further believe they have the special formula for preparing the 12 loaves of bread that must rest on the table.

The mizraq. This was a water pitcher used in the operation of the Jewish temple. Some are made of pure silver or gold. The Temple Institute has a number of *mizraqot* available already and continues to produce more.

Additional tools. Other tools already developed for use in the future Jewish temple include…

> the silver cup and the golden flask
> the incense chalice, which holds the ingredients for the
>   incense offering
> a silver shovel
> a lottery box, which contains the lots to be cast on the Day
>   of Atonement
> copper washbasins
> silver trumpets
> harps

All of these items have already been constructed and await the completion of the temple.

The Reformed Sanhedrin

Grant Jeffrey notes, "Before Israel can rebuild the Temple, the ancient Sanhedrin must be reestablished." He acknowledges the absence of this religious body since 453. However, "seventy-one of the most highly respected rabbis in Israel received special ordination as the new Sanhedrin on October 13, 2004. The new Sanhedrin includes Orthodox Jewish leaders from every part of Israel."[6]

> The current attempt to re-institute semicha and re-establish a Sanhedrin is the sixth attempt in the last five

hundred years, but unlike previous attempts, for the first time there seems to be wide consensus among the leading Torah sages living in the Land of Israel for the pressing need for such an institution at this time.[7]

This group of 70 male Jewish leaders is required for the future temple because only the Sanhedrin can select the man who will serve as the high priest of the temple. The word *Sanhedrin* comes from the Greek word *synedrion*, meaning a council or place of meeting. In the Bible, it refers to the governing body or supreme council of the Jews, which functioned as both a religious and civil court. The people stood before the Temple Mount to have their questions answered or their causes heard and decided by the smaller Sanhedrin (called the Lesser Sanhedrin) of 23 men who sat near the Greater Sanhedrin.

> The make-up of the council includes a President—*Nasi*, Chancellor—*Av beis din*, and sixty-nine general members who all sit in the form of a semi-circle when in session. Decisions are made by majority vote. The constitution of seventy-one is to preclude the possibility of a tie. Members of the Sanhedrin are not elected, nor is their position permanent. Any scholar, at any time, may gain a place on the legislature by proving a greater level of scholarship in Jewish Law than a current member of the legislature.[8]

Scholar Arnold Fruchtenbaum makes this note:

> The significance of Israel's reinstituting the Sanhedrin may be another event that leaves in place the possibility of how the Lord will work out His will with His people. Almost sixty years after a 1900-year absence, the nation of Israel came into existence. Jewish people from the four corners of the world have made *aliyah* to live in the Land. The Temple Institute in Jerusalem has reconstructed the

instruments for Jewish Temple worship; Jewish men determined to be descendants of Aaron, known as the *Kohanim*, are being trained in ritual practices to serve as Temple priests; and now we have the establishment of an authoritative body to speak to the nation of Israel on matters of Jewish religion. This is significant in light of such passages as Zechariah 12:10 and Hosea 5:15, which speak of a time when the people of Israel will be led into the acceptance of Jesus as their Messiah. The existence of a religious authority for the entire nation will facilitate the multitudes coming to faith.[9]

The origin of the Sanhedrin can be traced back to Moses, who appointed 70 men to assist him in his duties. In the time of Jesus, it was comprised of 71 members: 70 elders and scribes plus the high priest. This group usually met near the temple in Jerusalem. The Sanhedrin could issue sentences, but only the Roman procurator could ratify and carry out a death sentence. The Great Sanhedrin in Israel exercised supreme spiritual authority and settled all religious questions. The Sanhedrin was dismantled when Jerusalem was destroyed in AD 70. They reconvened after the fall of Jerusalem but never attained the same power.

The political power of the Sanhedrin varied based on political circumstances. Sometimes it was strong, but at other times the Sanhedrin ruled in name only. At the arrest of Jesus, the Sanhedrin held much sway. They condemned Jesus, collaborating with the Roman government to have Him put to death.

In Acts 22:30–23:10, the apostle Paul also stood before the Sanhedrin. When he mentioned his belief in the resurrection of the dead, the main two religious groups—the Pharisees and the Sadducees—quarreled so much that Paul had to be taken away for safety. The Jews then made a plot to kill Paul. When the plot was discovered, Paul was transferred to Governor Felix for his protection (Acts 23:12-33).

The Lost Ark

The one item of central importance in the original Jewish temple was the mysterious Ark of the Covenant. The source of films, novels, and untold speculations, this missing Ark has enticed adventurers around the world to search for it.

One legend states that the Ark is in Ethiopia. That rumor came about as a result of the Queen of Sheba's visit to King Solomon around 960 BC. In this fable, King Solomon was infatuated with the Queen and gave her the Ark to take back home. The Ark, ending up in Ethiopia almost 3000 years ago, has been handed down through the royal families for protection to the present day. This legend is still widely believed in Ethiopia but is rejected by virtually all other serious Jewish and Christian scholars.

Where is the Ark? The Bible may confirm the location of the Ark itself in 2 Chronicles 35:3—an account of an event that occurred prior to the dispersion of the Jewish people during the Babylonian captivity. The ruler of Judah, King Josiah, believed the temple would come under attack and instructed the Levites to "put the holy ark in the house" (2 Chronicles 35:3). He was not referring to the temple, but to the place King Solomon had previously prepared to keep the Ark safe. This is supported by two considerations. First, the Ark had been in Solomon's temple for almost 400 years when Josiah gave this command. King Solomon had built the temple and placed the Ark in the Holy of Holies around 964 BC (1 Kings 8:1-11).

Second, the Hebrew word used for *house* (*bayih*) means "a special place, a shelter, in the inward parts." Some believe this refers to a location *under* the Holy of Holies that today is found underneath the Dome of the Rock on the Temple Mount. For example, the Jewish Talmud makes this claim. Yet no one has been able to verify the location of the Ark. Wild rumors have suggested the Ark is in various places—taken to Egypt by Pharaoh Shishak, hidden under the Dome of the Rock, captured by the Crusaders and taken to the Vatican in Rome, or captured by the Muslims and taken to Mecca.

The proper biblical explanation is found in Revelation 11:19, where we read, "The temple of God was opened in heaven, and there was seen in his temple the ark of the testament." This passage clearly indicates that the prototype of the Ark is in heaven, superseding any earthly copy.

Any serious study of the Ark of the Covenant must also take into consideration Ezekiel 8–11, which indicates that the glory (Hebrew, *chabod*) of God departed from the Ark prior to the Babylonian destruction of Jerusalem in 586 BC. Even if someone were to find the golden box today, God's presence is no longer there. He departed long ago because the people of Jerusalem had turned their backs on Him. With no glory (Hebrew, *ichabod*), the city and temple were left defenseless. Even if someone were to find the Ark today it would be powerless. God's presence and power departed long ago.

A Possible International Solution

Even if the placement of the Jewish temple does not interfere with the existing Islamic holy sites, its construction could prove problematic because of the ongoing hostility between Jews and Muslims. An international settlement would have to be negotiated, possibly by someone with the skills of the coming Antichrist. In fact, the construction of the new temple may be a part of the peace treaty the Antichrist signs with Israel in Daniel 9:27.

Regardless of its proper location on the Temple Mount, the temple could be built without regard for the Islamic shrines if those sites are destroyed in a war (perhaps the war prophesied in Ezekiel 38–39), by an earthquake, or by terrorism. In any case, a new temple must be constructed no later than the midpoint of the tribulation because that is where the Antichrist will make his boastful demand for worship as God (2 Thessalonians 2:3-4).

But whatever happens, a Jewish temple will once again sit on the Temple Mount. The tragedy will be that the Antichrist will eventually turn against the people of Israel and go to that temple to demand the world worship him as God.

God will deal with the world severely in the time of the tribulation, when the wrath of the Lamb and the wrath of God are poured
out on unbelievers. But the judgments of God are intended to drive
people to cry out to Him one last time while there is still hope. God
is not sitting back saying, "I've just been waiting to do this." His
judgments come as an inevitable result of man's rejection of God
and the things of God.

The future of the Dome of the Rock, and indeed the entire Temple Mount, is in the hands of God. We believe a future Jewish temple will one day replace the Dome, but that does not mean we ought
to attempt to hasten this event. God Himself will cause this to happen in His own time and manner. In the meantime, we await His
determined purpose to bring about the fulfillment of this prophecy.

6

THE HOLOCAUST ECLIPSED

Jesus reminds us in Matthew 24:21 that there will come a time of great tribulation such as the world has never seen and never will see again. It will be worse even than the Nazi Holocaust against the Jews. We regret this and pray for the peace of Jerusalem (Psalm 122:6) even as we realize the gravity of Jesus's prediction.

Revelation 11:2 tells us that the Gentiles will trample on the holy city for 42 months, or three and a half years. Zechariah 14:2 describes the event this way: "For I will gather all nations against Jerusalem to battle; and the city shall be taken, and the houses rifled, and the women ravished; and half of the city shall go forth in captivity."

But then in verse 3 Zechariah says the Lord will go forth and fight against the nations that have attacked her. So we see that both Testaments predict a tragedy is coming for the people of Jerusalem. The Old Testament prophets were concerned that as the people of Israel turned their backs on God, they would eventually invite the judgment of God, which would involve Gentiles attacking the holy city and trying to destroy it. This has happened in the past—Romans, Muslims, and Christian Crusaders have attacked the city, but in none of these occasions did Christ return to deliver the city as the prophets predicted. Thus, these predictions are yet to be fulfilled.

The Scripture reminds us that several unique things will happen in the future. Many of the people of Israel will turn to the Lord during the time of tribulation. They will finally be convinced that the time of the end has come and that they need to acknowledge Jesus as the true Messiah.

But that's when the Antichrist, who hates the things of God and hates the true Messiah, will turn against the Jewish people and attack them. That's why I am so convinced that Christians should defend the nation and people of Israel—because God's hand is upon them in such a unique way. It is so unique, in fact, that as the prophet Isaiah said, eventually God Himself will come to earth to defend them.

That did not happen when the Babylonians attacked or when the Romans attacked. God did not intervene then and deliver the nation and people of Israel. That is yet to happen.

The End of the Age

When we talk about the age in which we live or the end of the age, the New Testament uses the Greek word *telos* ("end" or "completion")—the word from which we get the English word *telescope*. The end is the time of completion, and in the Scriptures, it always refers to the end of the times of the Gentiles, which includes the church age and the time of the tribulation. Jesus Himself made clear that until the times of the Gentiles are complete, the work of God for the nation and people of Israel is not finished. God will again turn His attention to Israel when the times of the Gentiles are complete.

In the meantime, Jesus viewed history as moving toward a final climax, not in endless cycles of repetition. He emphasized that when the current age comes to an end, another age will begin. The Old Testament Jews called this age the *hauolam hazzeh*, and they called the age to come the *hauolam habbah*. They understood that God was working in one age and one dispensation and that He would eventually work in another age and another dispensation. The present age will one day come to an end and be replaced by another.

As we study the Bible, we discover that that age to come is the millennial kingdom of Christ on earth. That age does not exist right now. Spiritually, in our hearts, we are citizens of the kingdom of heaven. We are in submission to the authority of Christ, who reigns and rules from heaven in the life of the believer. But we are not living in a literal kingdom of God on earth. God does not intend for Christians to try to establish a political theocracy. Every attempt to do that has ended in disaster. Instead, we are to live out the message of the gospel to the world, inviting people to faith in Jesus Christ and preparing them for the kingdom age to come and for eternity.

In the Old Testament, we find similar a concept in the expression *the latter days* (Hebrew, *beaharit hayyamim*). For example, in Deuteronomy 4:30-31, Moses foretold the future apostasy of the people of Israel, their scattering, and their return to the land in the latter days. The prophet Hosea predicted Israel's future repentance in the latter days (Hosea 3:5). Jeremiah and Ezekiel also predicted numerous events that would happen in the latter days and the latter years (Jeremiah 23:20; Ezekiel 38:8).

So both Old Testament prophets and New Testament preachers looked down through the corridor of time and foresaw something coming in the future. They reminded their generations, "Understand the times in which you live, and understand what's coming in the future." So, what exactly is coming for the future?

Great Tribulation

In the Olivet Discourse, Jesus's longest prophetic message, He said, "For then shall be great tribulation, such as was not since the beginning of the world to this time, no, nor ever shall be" (Matthew 24:21). Jesus predicted the tribulation would be worse than the Nazi Holocaust, which was yet to come, and worse than Israel's persecution in Egypt before the exodus, which was in the past. This is something greater than all of that. This time of great tribulation is yet to occur. It will be a time of the end of the present age, the final culmination of the wrath of God on the world, setting the stage for the age that is yet to come.

Jesus taught that the tribulation would include the "abomination of desolation, spoken of by Daniel the prophet" (Matthew 24:15). He was referring to Daniel 9, where Daniel predicted that the Antichrist would come and desecrate a future temple and that the judgment of God would fall like never before in history.

Some people say, "Well, that happened when Antiochus Epiphanes came to Jerusalem and desecrated the second temple." But Jesus indicated that this is yet to happen. Other people say, "This happened when the Romans destroyed the second temple in AD 70." But Jesus predicted the time of tribulation would culminate in His triumphal return in power and great glory. This is the return that the apostle Paul calls "the glorious appearing of the great God and our Savior Jesus Christ" when He comes to rule and reign on earth. That did not happen in AD 70. The sun and the moon were not darkened. The stars did not fall. The heavens were not shaken. Jesus did not return.

Finally, some say, "Well, that's just apocalyptic language about the future." But as Jesus looked down through the corridor of time, He described a literal event. Matthew 24 finds its parallel in Revelation 16, where we read of the terrible judgments of God that will fall in the end times—in the tribulation that is yet to come. The wrath of God will be poured out on the earth, on the sea, on the rivers, and on the sun. Great ecological disasters will bring the planet to the brink of extinction. The description of the final hour of the tribulation includes atmospheric darkness, air pollution, ecological disasters, and cataclysmic events. The book of Revelation pictures these as the judgments of the seals, trumpets, and bowls. Twenty-one judgments are coming in the future that will shake the planet, bring it to its knees, and ultimately bring in the kingdom of God on earth.

Judgment on Unbelievers

The Bible clearly outlines two purposes of the tribulation period. The first is to judge unbelievers. Over and over, the book of Revelation focuses on unbelievers who refuse to repent. They shake their fists in God's face and continue to reject Him in spite of what is happening.

A lot of people think, "If the world really were about to blow up, and everything were to go wrong, I would get saved. I would give my life to Christ." Yet the book of Revelation reveals that most of those who live during the coming tribulation will believe lies, will be deceived, will not repent, and will not come to faith (Revelation 9:20; 16:11).

Trust me, you do not want to be left behind. Everything will go wrong! The wrath of Christ, the wrath of God, and even the wrath of Satan will be poured out in the time that Jesus described as "great tribulation." It is not just a time of normal persecution or normal trouble. The church has always faced persecution, trouble, difficulties, and even martyrdom. But when the tribulation period begins, divine wrath will be poured out on an unbelieving world. We can be thankful the church is not the object of that wrath.

The Time of Jacob's Trouble

Second, the tribulation will be "the time of Jacob's trouble" (Jeremiah 30:7). It has a special purpose for the people and nation of Israel. This is not Christian prejudice being read into the Bible. The Old Testament prophets clearly warned their own people, the people of Israel, that trouble was coming. In fact, the prophet Joel said armies will surround Jerusalem at the time of the end. The prophet Zechariah looked down through the halls of history and warned his countrymen that two-thirds of the people of Israel will be slaughtered in a future time of tribulation (Zechariah 13:8). At the same time, he predicted the salvation of one third of the Jews, a remnant of true believers, who will put their faith in the coming Messiah (verse 9).

The tribulation period is designed to accomplish several things.

- The rapture of the church, which precipitates the

tribulation, will demonstrate to the people of Israel that the Bible is true and that they have been left behind.

- God will then empower two witnesses to come on the scene (likely two prominent Jewish leaders) to proclaim the message that Jesus truly is the promised Messiah (Revelation 11).

- Then 144,000 believers—12,000 from each of the 12 tribes of Israel—will spread the same message and try to evangelize the people who were left behind (Revelation 7:4-8).

Hope for the Future

The Bible gives us words of hope for what is going to happen in the future. A host of Gentiles will be saved. A number of Jews will be saved. But trouble is coming, and the vast majority of the world's population will be lost.

These prophecies scare the daylights out of people. They cause people to say, "Well, I don't want to know. I don't really like Bible prophecy. It really frightens me. You're telling me that trees are going to burn up, grass is going to burn up, the air is going to be polluted, judgment is going to fall, the wrath of God is going to fall…Is there any hope for the future at all?"

Of course there is. And the Bible tells us exactly what that hope is. The apostle Paul expressed it perhaps best in his clear word to Titus that we are to be "looking for that blessed hope, and the glorious appearing of the great God and our Savior, Jesus Christ" (Titus 2:13).

The message of prophecy is not just a message of the judgment to come. That is for the unbeliever. But for the believer, the message of the coming of Christ is the blessed hope that He is coming back for His own to take us home to heaven itself. Jesus said His second coming would be marked by "the sign of the Son of man" (Matthew 24:30).

Commentators through the centuries have tried to guess what that sign will be. Chrysostom suggested it will be the sign of the cross. Lang said it will be the Shekinah glory. The fact is that one day, the sign will appear and Christ will return. The assumption is that this glorious appearing will happen after the seven-year tribulation period and that all will see it. But the speculation is vast. Is it the Bethlehem star? Is it the cross? Is it the blood moon? Is it the Shekinah glory? Whatever form it might take, it is the splendor of Christ Himself appearing in the future. And then it will be obvious what it is all about. The hope of the future is not in understanding all of the details. The hope of the future is in understanding the promise.

When Jesus ascended into heaven, the disciples were stunned. As the risen Savior went back to heaven, they stood staring up into the sky, watching Him go. And we read this incredible statement from two angels to the disciples: "Ye men of Galilee, why stand ye gazing up into heaven? this same Jesus, which is taken up from you into heaven, shall so come in like manner as ye have seen him go into heaven" (Acts 1:11).

In other words, the hope of the believer for the future is that this same Jesus will return. How did He ascend into heaven? Literally, bodily, and physically. How will He return one day? Literally, bodily, and physically. At the rapture (the blessed hope), He will come in the clouds to take the church home to the marriage in heaven. And after the marriage (at the glorious appearing), we will accompany Him in His triumphal return to the earth. The hope of Scripture is that Jesus is coming again.

The apostle Paul referred to this event when teaching about the communion service: "For as often as ye eat this bread, and drink this cup, ye do show the Lord's death till he come" (1 Corinthians 11-26). Every communion service anticipates the coming of Christ. Those who would argue that the prophecies of the coming of Christ have already been fulfilled would also have to explain why we continue to have communion services. They are to continue until He comes. No,

He has not yet come. We celebrate communion to remember not only that He died and rose again but also that He is coming again.

Paul writes to the Thessalonians that wherever he went, people talked about how they "turned to God from idols to serve the living and true God; and to wait for his Son from heaven, whom he raised from the dead, even Jesus, which delivered us from the wrath to come" (1 Thessalonians 1:9-10). What wrath to come? The wrath that comes in the time of the tribulation. The believer is not anticipating the wrath but looking for the Savior. He is not awaiting the Antichrist. He is looking for Jesus Christ. Some of us are not even expecting the undertaker; we are looking for the upper-taker.

Second Thessalonians 1:10 says, "He shall come to be glorified in his saints." When Christ comes in the rapture to take the saints home to heaven, He will be glorified in them. But the return of Christ in power, glory, and judgment on the world comes after the time of tribulation. Paul put it this way in 1 Timothy 6:14-15: "That thou keep this commandment without spot, unrebukeable, until the appearing of our Lord Jesus Christ: which in his times he shall show [that is, in the proper time, God will make evident], who is the blessed and only Potentate, the King of kings, and Lord of lords."

That is what we have in the book of Revelation, when the Lamb is identified as the coming King. With the climactic proclamation in Revelation 19, heaven opens. The rider on the white horse comes forth with the sword of His mouth, the power of His spoken word (verses 11-16). Jesus returns with those who are robed in white from the marriage. He comes back with the church—no longer the church rejected, persecuted, martyred, and trampled under. Now, the church triumphant marches out of heaven with her warrior Husband to reign and rule on the earth.

That is the message of hope for our future. The final chapters of the Bible remind us that Jesus is coming again. The church will ultimately triumph. Whatever the failures, problems, and struggles of earth are, all of them will be swept aside by the power and the glory of the triumphal return of Christ, who comes with the church to be glorified in His saints. He comes with His saints in glory and power to reign and rule on the earth, and He is revealed as the true leader of the world: the King of kings, the Lord of lords.

The book of Hebrews sums it up when it says, "So Christ was once offered to bear the sins of many; and unto them that look for him shall he appear the second time without sin unto salvation" (Hebrews 9:28). Jesus came the first time to die for our sins. He is coming the second time to take His family home to heaven and then to reign and rule in righteousness. The Bridegroom is coming to the bride. The Bridegroom is coming to reign and rule ultimately on the earth. That is the promise of Scripture.

The message of the gospel—the death, burial, and resurrection of Christ—is tied to the great prediction of the return of Christ. When this age is done and the work of God has been complete for the church age, when the tribulation judgments are finished, when Israel has come to faith in the Messiah, then the Lord Himself will return. Israel will be delivered. Christ will reign and rule on earth. Hallelujah—the Lamb shall become the King! All Israel will proclaim, "Blessed is he that cometh in the name of the Lord" (Matthew 23:39).

7

GOD COMES TO EARTH

The seventh future event that will shake the world is Jesus's return to earth. The Lord Himself will descend to the Mount of Olives and split that mountain in half (Zechariah 14:4). That has never happened throughout history. I have been to the Mount of Olives a dozen times. It is still intact. It has never split in half. That is yet to occur.

Of course, the New Testament speaks about this event as well. In Revelation 19, we find that triumphant passage about the return of Christ. Remember, in the rapture, the believers go up to heaven to the marriage with Christ, "the marriage of the Lamb" (verses 7-9). In the return, we come back with Christ in the judgment at the Battle of Armageddon.

> And I saw heaven opened, and behold a white horse; and he that sat upon him was called Faithful and True, and in righteousness he doth judge and make war. His eyes were like a flame of fire, and on his head were many crowns; and he had a name written, that no man knew, but he himself (verses 11-12).

That is the secret, unspoken name of God. But we also read that "his name is called The Word of God" (verse 13). The Scripture makes it clear that Jesus Himself is the living Word, who comes from heaven at the time of the second coming, at the time of the deliverance of the city of Jerusalem. "And the armies which were in heaven followed him upon white horses, clothed in fine linen, white and clean" (verse 14).

As we read the whole book of Revelation, it is obvious that this is the church, the bride of Christ. In verse 8, believers received white robes at the marriage of the Lamb. In verse 14, they ride out of heaven. They are no longer the church persecuted, rejected, martyred, or maligned. Instead, the bride of Christ rides out of heaven with her warrior Husband as the church triumphant at the time of the return of Christ.

> And out of his mouth goeth a sharp sword, that with it he should smite the nations: and he shall rule them with a rod of iron: and he treadeth the winepress of the fierceness and wrath of Almighty God. And he hath on his vesture and on his thigh a name written, KING OF KINGS, AND LORD OF LORDS (verses 15-16).

The triumph is that God Himself comes down to the earth in the person of Christ. The beast and the false prophet are cast alive into the lake of fire. Satan is bound in the abyss. Jesus rules with His saints for 1000 years on earth and then in eternity.

The whole hope of the message of the Bible is that God has not abandoned the earth. God Himself will come one day. At the final moment, when hope seems lost, Christ will return and save the world from destruction. He Himself will destroy the enemy and set up His kingdom on earth.

Let's take a closer look at when Jesus comes back at His final, triumphal return. Scripture reveals signs of His coming, a sequence of events, and the supremacy of His rule.

The Bible is filled with hundreds of amazing prophecies, but the greatest prophecy is that of the second coming of Jesus Christ. More than 300 prophecies point to the fact that Jesus is coming again. These will be fulfilled literally at the time of Christ's return.

Signs of His Coming

Near the end of Jesus's earthly ministry, His disciples asked Him several questions about the future. They wanted to know when He would return and what signs would precede His return and the end of the world. Jesus answered their question about the sign of His coming by saying, "Then shall be great tribulation, such as was not since the beginning of the world to this time, no, nor ever shall be" (Matthew 24:21).

This coming tribulation will be worse than any world war we have experienced, worse than the Nazi Holocaust (as we saw in chapter 6), and worse than any of the great cataclysmic judgments of the past. A time of trouble is coming that the Bible identifies as the tribulation period. It is "the time of Jacob's trouble" (Jeremiah 30:7). After the rapture of the church to heaven, all hell will break loose on the earth.

Jesus continued to answer their question about the sign of His coming.

> Immediately after the tribulation of those days shall the sun be darkened, and the moon shall not give her light, and the stars shall fall from heaven, and the powers of the heavens shall be shaken: and then shall appear the sign of the Son of man in heaven (Matthew 24:29-30).

Jesus is assuring His disciples that no one will miss the sign of His coming. Everybody will know that He is coming back. The sign will appear in the heavens. "And then shall all the tribes of the earth mourn, and they shall see the Son of man coming in the clouds of heaven with power and great glory" (verse 30).

The New Testament affirms that Christ's coming is imminent—there are no signs that must occur first, and the rapture could occur at any moment. We are to keep watching for Jesus to come for His own. But after the tribulation, when He returns to earth to judge the world and set up His kingdom on the earth, the sign of the Son of Man will appear in the heavens.

Scholars have debated over the years what the sign will be. The Bible does not make that clear. But it does make clear that when it happens, it will be so obvious that nobody will miss it. Everyone will see Jesus coming in the clouds in power and in great glory. That never happened in the past—it is yet to happen in the future. This is what the Bible calls the "glorious appearing of Christ," the epiphany of Christ. It is the shining glory of the radiance of His presence when He returns. The entire world will see Him when He comes back.

Jesus ends that message in Matthew 24 with a whole series of challenges. He says in verse 32, "Learn a parable of the fig tree." When its branches are tender and it puts forth leaves, it is going to put forth fruit. You know that summer is coming. So likewise, when you see all these things (not some of them, but all of them), you can know that His coming is near, "even at the doors" (verse 33).

Remember the distinction between the rapture, when we go up in the clouds, and the return, when we come back with the Lord. There are no signs for the rapture. The signs are for the return, the second coming of Christ.

The Bible gives us constant reminders that Jesus indeed is coming again. He promised the disciples when He left them, "If I go and prepare a place for you, I will come again, and receive you unto myself" (John 14:3). In fact, the doctrine of the second coming of Christ is so clearly stated in the New Testament, it is included in the doctrinal statement of virtually all Christian denominations of the world. They may differ on when and how He will come, but they all agree that one day, Christ will return again. The message in this passage is that He will come when all these signs are fulfilled in one generation.

Beginning in Matthew 24:36, Jesus goes on to say that nobody knows the day or the hour. The day of His coming will be like the days of Noah, when people were eating and drinking and doing their own thing, completely unaware of the purpose, person, and power of God. Judgment came suddenly and swept them all away. So shall the coming of the Son of Man be.

Jesus also reminds us that the generation that sees all these things will not pass "till all these things be fulfilled" (verse 34). All of those signs did not occur in His generation, in the first century, or throughout church history. They are yet to come. They will all culminate at one time, at the time of the end, when every one of those 300 prophecies about the second coming of Christ finally reaches its climax. When all these signs appear, Christ's coming will be "at the doors." Jesus counsels His disciples to "watch therefore" (verse 42), to "be ye also ready" (verse 44), and to keep serving like the "faithful and wise servant" (verse 45).

Jesus assured the disciples, "I am leaving you and going back to heaven, but I will return." Later, as the disciples watched Him ascend into heaven, two angels appeared and also assured them, "This same Jesus, which is taken up from you into heaven, shall so come in like manner as ye have seen him go into heaven" (Acts 1:11).

The Sequence of Events

The sign of Jesus's coming will appear at the end of the tribulation period, when it is finally too late for people to call on Him and turn to Him. It will be the sign of the glorious appearing of Christ Himself, who comes in the Shekinah glory to judge the world and to set up His kingdom on earth. That is going to be an ominous time. A sequence of events in Revelation 19 describes it. In verse 11, we read of the return of the Son of God Himself: "And I saw heaven opened, and behold a white horse; and he that sat upon him was called Faithful and True, and in righteousness he doth judge and make war."

When Jesus comes in the rapture, He will come suddenly for His own, to call the church home to heaven with a trumpet and a shout.

We will be out of here to the glory of God. But when He comes in the return, the sign of the coming of Christ will be seen by the whole world. The tribes of the earth will mourn because He is coming, and He will make war against the Antichrist.

"His eyes were as a flame of fire, and on his head were many crowns; and he had a name written, that no man knew, but he himself" (Revelation 19:12). This is the secret, unspoken name of God. "And he was clothed with a vesture dipped in blood: and his name is called The Word of God" (verse 13). Remember, John, "the disciple whom Jesus loved," wrote the book of Revelation. He also wrote the Gospel and three epistles that bear his name. In his Gospel, in the epistle of 1 John, and in the book of Revelation, he describes Christ as "the Word of God." Any first-century believer reading Revelation 19:13 would have understood immediately that this is Jesus, who is riding out of heaven as the conquering King on the white horse.

Verse 14 then declares, "And the armies which were in heaven followed him upon white horses, clothed in fine linen, white and clean." We read in verses 7-8 that this army received their white linen robes at the marriage of the Lamb. This is not an army of angels, though angels may attend them. This is the raptured church, riding out of heaven in triumph. This is the bride of Christ being put on display back on earth, where she will reign and rule with Christ. This is your future destiny. I have circled verse 14 in my Bible and drawn an arrow pointing to it. You might even want to put your name in the margin, or at least write the word *me* there—with an exclamation point!

This is your future destiny. Regardless of how old you are, you have more living ahead of you than you do behind you. The rapture, the judgment seat of Christ, the marriage with the Lamb, the triumphal return, the millennial kingdom, and an eternity of joyful service to God are all ahead of you. Right now, we are just warming up. Our time on earth is a practice run, preparing us for our return with Christ and eternal life with Him.

The passage comes to this great climax in the triumphal return of Christ: "And out of his mouth goeth a sharp sword, that with it he should smite the nations: and he shall rule them with a rod of iron: and he treadeth the winepress of the fierceness and wrath of Almighty God. And he hath on his vesture and on his thigh a name written, KING OF KINGS, AND LORD OF LORDS" (verses 15-16). The sharp sword is a symbol of His spoken word. The church comes with Him—no longer the church rejected, no longer the church persecuted, martyred, and maligned. Now she is the church triumphant, who marches out of heaven with her warrior Husband to reign and rule on the earth.

All of this prophecy points to this powerful time, the triumphal return of Christ. Jesus came the first time humbly and quietly, born in a stable in Bethlehem to Mary and His adopted father, Joseph. He came into the world as a humble rabbi, preaching a message of repentance and the kingdom of heaven. Had the people of Israel repented and received the King, they would have received the kingdom as well. But they did not repent or accept the King. They rejected the King and lost the opportunity to enter into the kingdom. But it is not lost forever.

The Bible makes clear that every person who comes by faith to Christ becomes a spiritual citizen of that kingdom. The kingdom of Christ can become a reality in your own heart and life. The Bible also tells us that one day the kingdom will be a literal reality on earth. For when the King returns, He will set up the kingdom.

After 40 years in the ministry, I am convinced that the church is never going to bring in the kingdom of God on the earth by itself. The kingdom will literally exist on this earth only when the King comes back. That is the promise of Scripture. That is the hope of the believer—that the King is indeed coming again.

Supremacy of His Rule

We have seen that Jesus Himself announced the sign of His coming—the glorious appearing, the epiphany of Christ, when He returns to reign and rule on the earth. Then we looked at the sequence of events in Revelation 19 that will happen when Christ marches out of heaven with the great army of the raptured church to reign and rule on earth, when the grand procession brings in the kingdom of heaven to earth itself. Now we want to examine the supremacy of His rule.

At the end of Revelation 19, Jesus returns, speaks the word, and the Battle of Armageddon is over almost before it begins. It is a battle that is not really a battle. The Bible says He slew the army of the Antichrist with the sword of His mouth, the power of His spoken word (verse 21).

The Savior, who spoke the creation into existence, speaks again, and all resistance is gone. He takes the beast and the false prophet and casts them alive into the lake of fire (verse 20). Sin is judged, Satan is bound in the abyss for 1000 years, and Christ and the saints reign and rule in a literal millennial kingdom on earth.

What will that be like? The prophet Isaiah gives us a description of that kingdom in the very last chapter of his book. It is quite similar to what is presented in the book of Revelation. "For, behold, the LORD will come with fire, and with his chariots like a whirlwind, to render his anger with fury, and his rebuke with flames of fire. For by fire and by his sword will the LORD plead with all flesh: and the slain of the LORD shall be many" (Isaiah 66:15-16).

This is the same event described in Revelation 19. When Christ the Lord returns, He will slay the army of the Antichrist and then set up His kingdom. Then Isaiah says, "For I know their works and their thoughts: it shall come, that I will gather all nations and tongues; and they shall come, and see my glory. And I will set a sign among them, and I will send those that escape of them unto the nations" (Isaiah 66:18-19).

This passage refers to those who escape out of the nations and survive the tribulation judgments. Isaiah names the places they come from and then says, "And they shall declare my glory among the Gentiles" (verse 19).

Isaiah was a Jewish prophet. The Jewish people believed that the Lord Himself would someday come and set up a kingdom on earth and declare His glory to the Jews. But here Isaiah, the Jewish prophet, makes it clear that the Lord will also declare His glory to the Gentiles—those who had been unbelievers but who will come to know who He is.

Verses 20-21 and 23 add, "And they shall bring all your brethren for an offering unto the Lord out of all nations…to my holy mountain Jerusalem, saith the Lord…And I will also take of them for priests and for Levites, saith the Lord…And from one sabbath to another, shall all flesh come to worship before me, saith the Lord." Isaiah foresaw a time when the kingdom of heaven would come and God would rule on the earth. God the Father, the Bible tells us, is a Spirit (John 4:24). No man at any time has seen God the Father (John 1:18). But God the Son has taken on an incarnate human form in the person of Jesus Christ. He appeared in the Old Testament as "the angel of the Lord." He appeared in the New Testament as the baby born in Bethlehem. He was destined to go to the cross, to die for our sins, and to rise from the dead. He will return one day to reign and rule in person on the earth.

The Old Testament prophets made it clear that God will come one day. How else could He come? He comes in human form to rule through the person of Jesus Christ. The Bible shouts to us about the deity of Jesus Christ. He is not just a humble rabbi, a good man, or a great teacher who is trying to show us the way to God. No, this is the Son of God, God Himself, incarnate in human flesh.

We struggle to understand and comprehend the triune nature of God, who is Father, Son, and Spirit. Yet the Bible makes it very clear that the Son of God is God Himself. Jesus has all of the characteristics and attributes of deity. He will come to bring the kingdom of God to earth to reign and rule. He is indeed, as Isaiah the prophet said, Emmanuel, God with us.

That's why Jesus would dare to say that He has the power to

forgive our sins. Some scribes and Pharisees heard Him and asked, "Why doth this man thus speak blasphemies? who can forgive sins but God only?" But Jesus later said to His disciples, "He that hath seen Me hath seen the Father" (John 14:9). He told a crowd of Jews, "I and my Father are one" (John 10:30). He shouts to us of His deity. He declares it. In the supremacy of His rule, He will reign and rule as God on earth in a millennial kingdom that is yet to come, when the lion, the lamb, the wolf, the bear, and the ox will all lie down with one another. Nature will be at peace. People will be at peace because Christ will be on the throne.

What a day that is going to be! What a wonderful time of blessing, peace, and prosperity beyond anything the world has ever known! But that will be a reality only for those who believe in Him. In part 2 we will discuss five prophetic signs that reveal this future in greater detail as we continue our look at 15 future events that will shake the world.

FIVE SIGNS
THAT REVEAL THE FUTURE

Questions about the future are not new. People have always wondered, "What is going to happen in the days ahead? Does the Bible reveal anything about future events?" The Bible contains more than 300 prophecies of the second coming of Christ. It also contains 109 prophecies of the first coming of Christ. All 109 of the prophecies of the first coming were literally fulfilled in the life and times of Jesus. That should give us confidence that the 300 prophecies of the second coming will also be literally fulfilled in the future. In part 2 we will look at five prophetic signs that reveal the future and tell us we are clearly moving closer to the time of the end.

As Jesus approached the final days before He went to the cross, He made this statement:

> There shall be signs in the sun, and in the moon, and in the stars; and upon the earth distress of nations, with perplexity; the sea and the waves roaring; men's hearts failing them for fear, and for looking after those things which are coming on the earth: for the powers of heaven shall be shaken. And then shall they see the Son of man coming in a cloud with power and great glory. And when these things begin to come to pass, then look up, and lift up your heads; for your redemption draweth nigh (Luke 21:25-28).

In other words, Jesus was reminding us that the whole world would someday see signs of His coming. We have seen that there will be no signs for the rapture of the church. That could happen at any moment. The trumpet could sound, the archangel could shout, and we could be called home to glory to be with the Lord. In contrast, Scripture describes definite signs that will precede the return of Christ to the earth.

I like to look at it like this. If I visited the mall in autumn and saw Christmas decorations, I would know that Christmas was coming. But that would also mean Thanksgiving must be coming as well because it comes before Christmas. Similarly, if I see signs of the return of Christ, I know that the rapture is even nearer.

People have said for years, "We're moving closer to the time of the end, and we think we see the signs of the second coming." Why am I so convinced that we may be the generation on the verge of the return of Christ? I want to share five suggestions from Scripture itself, five undeniable signs that reveal the future. These five signs clearly indicate that God's end-time clock is ticking and that time is racing toward a final date with divine destiny.

8

THE RETURN OF ISRAEL

After 19 centuries of being expelled from the land of Israel, the Jews returned to form a nation in 1948. They are planted again back in their own homeland. Every Bible prophecy of future events assumes Israel will exist as a nation in the last days. But for about 19 centuries, that was not the case. A few Jewish people remained, but Israel did not exist as a nation until only about 65 years ago. The political entity was born in one day in a declaration of independence by a decision of the United Nations.

The prophet Isaiah, in the final chapter of his book, gives us one of the most amazing verses in the entire Bible. "Who hath heard such a thing? who hath seen such things? Shall the earth be made to bring forth in one day? or shall a nation be born at once? for as soon as Zion travailed, she brought forth her children" (Isaiah 66:8).

Both Christian and Jewish scholars acknowledge this passage is a prediction of Israel's rebirth in the land instantaneously—a nation born in a day. It had never happened in all of history. Never before had any nation or ethnic group been expelled from their land and then returned after nearly 2000 years with their language and heritage intact.

The very fact that Israel exists today is evidence that Bible prophecy is true. It demonstrates that God is real and that He has the power to fulfill what He has said will happen in the future. The return of Israel is a supersign of the end times. The prophecy has already been fulfilled. Israel has returned.

But what if the Jews were to be expelled from the land again because of unbelief? According to the Bible, this will not occur. We read in the Bible that God would bring Israel back the second time and plant them there permanently, never to be removed again (Isaiah 11:11-12). The first time, they returned from the Babylonian captivity and were replanted in the land. They were expelled when the Romans destroyed Jerusalem in AD 70. The second return occurred in the twentieth century, when Israel became a nation in a day. That alone should capture our attention and tell us we are moving closer to the time of the end.

The prophet Ezekiel also spoke of this rebirth of Israel. His prophecies clearly note Israel's return to life, to the land, and to the Lord.

Israel's Return to Life

Like Isaiah, Ezekiel foresaw a time when the nation of Israel would one day return to life.

> For I will take you from among the heathen, and gather you out of all countries, and will bring you into your own land. Then will I sprinkle clean water upon you, and ye shall be clean: from all your filthiness, and from all your idols, will I cleanse you. A new heart also will I give you, and a new spirit will I put within you: and I will take away the stony heart out of your flesh, and I will give you an heart of flesh. And I will put my spirit within you, and cause you to walk in my statutes, and ye shall keep my judgments, and do them. And ye shall dwell in the land that I gave your fathers; and ye shall be my people, and I will be your God (Ezekiel 36:24-28).

When Ezekiel was writing, Israel had been devastated by the Babylonians, and he himself had been taken into captivity. Yet he said a time would come when a nation that appeared to be dead would come back to life under the providence and care of God. God has not abandoned His people. Even though they may appear to be under judgment, He still has a plan and a purpose for them.

Then Ezekiel gives that famous prediction of the valley of dry bones. "The hand of the LORD was upon me, and carried me out in the spirit of the LORD, and set me down in the midst of the valley which was full of bones" (Ezekiel 37:1). The bones symbolize the nation of Israel, which appeared to be dead and scattered throughout the world.

"And caused me to pass by them round about: and, behold, there were very many in the open valley; and, lo, they were very dry" (verse 2). In other words, they had been there for a long time.

"And he said unto me, Son of man, can these bones live? And I answered, O Lord GOD, thou knowest" (verse 3). What is the answer? "Again he said unto me, Prophesy upon these bones, and say unto them, O ye dry bones, hear the word of the LORD" (verse 4).

Then Ezekiel says that as he preached to the bones, he heard a rattling sound, and the bones began to come together. The old spiritual "Dry Bones," which illustrates bones joining together, comes from this passage of Scripture, in which the bones of the skeletons suddenly begin to assemble right in front of the prophet's eyes.

Then he says in verses 7 and 8 that as he prophesied and the bones came together, flesh and sinews formed upon them, but there was no breath in them—no real spiritual life.

> Then said he unto me, Prophesy unto the wind, prophesy, son of man, and say to the wind, Thus saith the Lord GOD; Come from the four winds, O breath, and breathe upon these slain, that they may live. So I prophesied as he commanded me, and the breath came into them, and they lived, and stood up upon their feet, an exceeding great army (verses 9-10).

The interpretation of that part of the prophecy is obvious. Ezekiel is preaching to dry bones in a desert valley. Suddenly the bones assemble and come together, and they stand up. But they have no real life until the breath of God enters them. At that point, they are suddenly alive—not only physically but also spiritually.

Then God explains to Ezekiel the meaning of the vision: "Son of man, these bones are the whole house of Israel" (verse 11). That is the entire explanation of the prophecy of the valley of the dry bones. The dry bones represent the house of Israel and its people.

This is a prophecy about Israel's destiny. It's not about the church. The prophecy may be being fulfilled in our era, as Israel has returned to the land and the "bones" are being reassembled. According to the Word of God, Israel, the nation that was politically reborn in one day will someday be spiritually reborn as well.

Israel's Return to the Land

Then Ezekiel goes on to describe in detail the rest of the emphasis of that prophecy. He saw a time coming when the people of Israel would come back to life, come back to the land, and be reborn in the land. Israel would have its own Independence Day and celebrate its establishment as a new nation—a gift from God Himself. We know that this occurred in 1948, when the nation of Israel, against all odds, was suddenly born again in a day. The nation that was dead for 1900 years suddenly returned to life.

The question is, if Israel returned to the land, is God promising that they will remain in the land and that He will forever bless them in the land? Or will they continue to face difficulties and challenges in the land, just as they have throughout their history? In other words, what is ahead for the nation and people of Israel as they return to the land?

The prediction that Israel would one day return to the land is one of the great prophecies of the Old Testament. For centuries, some people said, "Oh, they'll never go back. They're scattered all over the world. How could you think God would bring the Jews back to the land of Israel, back to the Promised Land?"

However, the Jewish people themselves understood that promise because it is stated so clearly in Isaiah 11. There the prophet Isaiah also looks down through the halls of history into the distant future and discusses the millennial kingdom. He prophesies of the coming Messiah as a descendant of Jesse, David's father. The prophet also describes the sevenfold Spirit of the Lord resting on the Messiah:

> And there shall come forth a rod out of the stem of Jesse, and a Branch shall grow out of his roots. And the spirit of the LORD shall rest upon him, the spirit of wisdom and understanding, the spirit of counsel and might, the spirit of knowledge and of the fear of the LORD (Isaiah 11:1-2).

This is the sevenfold plenitude of the Spirit of God, the seven Spirits of Revelation 1:4. In the symbolism of the book of Revelation, the seven Spirits were there before the throne of God. These are not seven Holy Spirits. There is only one Holy Spirit. But Isaiah presents the sevenfold description of the Spirit—the Spirit of the Lord, of wisdom and understanding, of counsel and might, and of the knowledge and fear of the Lord. God would do something spiritually powerful. The Branch is the Messiah. He will come in the future out of the root of Jesse and David. A descendant of King David—Jesus of Nazareth, the Messiah—is the promised Savior.

Isaiah 11:4 confirms, "But with righteousness shall he judge the poor, and reprove with equity for the meek of the earth: and he shall smite the earth with the rod of his mouth, and with the breath of his lips shall he slay the wicked." This is the very same picture we have again in the book of Revelation: Christ will literally come one day to reign and rule on the earth.

Then Isaiah describes a wonderful time when the lion, the lamb, the wolf, and the calf will all lie down with one another—a time of peace and prosperity (verses 6-8). He looks ahead to the distant future and sees the coming of the Messiah and His reign in the future millennial kingdom. But then he says, "And in that day there shall be a root of Jesse, which shall stand for an ensign of the people; to it shall the Gentiles seek" (verse 10).

An ensign is a banner, and "the people" refers to the Jews. Isaiah then says, "And he shall set up an ensign for the nations [the Gentiles]" (verse 12). In other words, the Savior is coming for the Jews and for the Gentiles. He is the banner of God's love over both of them. He is the One who calls us to faith in the Lord God Jehovah.

But here is the key verse: "And it shall come to pass in that day, that the Lord shall set his hand again the second time to recover the remnant of his people" (verse 11). God brought the Jewish people back from the Babylonian captivity and restored them until the first coming of the Messiah. That was the first recovering of the remnant of his people. But they were scattered again by the Romans, and Scripture says God will recover His people a second time—this time from Assyria, Egypt, Pathros, Cush, Elam, Shinar, Hamath—and He will set up the Messiah as an ensign for the nations.

So Isaiah predicted that God would gather the people of Israel and bring them back into the land the second time. Today we see the fulfillment of that prediction as the Jewish people continue to go back to Israel, back to the Promised Land itself. They see themselves as fulfilling that prophecy. This return to the land is important to the heart, mind, and soul of the Jewish people.

If you are a Jewish reader, let me share a word from my heart to yours. God has called your nation to be a unique people unto Himself. God has blessed your people and sustained them through great difficulties as a nation throughout the centuries. But He is also calling you to faith in Himself. It is not enough to say, "We'll rebuild the nation by our political prowess, our military might, and our intellectual ingenuity." No. God may use all of those, but ultimately, if the Lord builds the house, it will stand. If He doesn't, it will not.

According to this prediction, Israel would come back to the land a second time (and they have been there since 1948), and then God will fulfill all His promises to the nation and people of Israel. People frequently ask me, "Don't you think Israel could suffer devastation and judgment and be scattered again?" Humanly speaking, that's certainly possible. But spiritually speaking, the Bible makes it very clear that once they are gathered a second time, they will never be scattered worldwide again. However, the Antichrist will attempt to drive them out.

The Bible predicts war will break out in the Middle East and Israel will be chased into the wilderness. There will be difficulties to face in the days ahead. But in God's unconditional covenant with Abraham, God promised to give the land to Israel. God is in the process of fulfilling that promise for the nation and people of Israel. However, just as important is God's promise that the Jewish people would return not only to life and to the land but also to the Lord.

Israel's Return to the Lord

The prophecies of the rebirth of the nation of Israel center on three elements: their return to life, their return to the land, and their ultimate return to the Lord Himself. That may sound strange to Jewish people. They might respond, "We've always believed in God—Jehovah, the God of the Bible, Yahweh Himself, the Lord and Savior, the God of Israel, the God of Abraham, Isaac, and Jacob." That may be true intellectually and theologically, but the real issue is, do you believe in Him personally, spiritually? Is He Lord and God and Savior in your life in a personal way?

As we read the Old Testament, the Hebrew Scriptures, we discover that sometimes the people of Israel loved the Lord their God and followed Him, and sometimes they did not. When they turned away from God, they came under the judgment of God as a result.

One of the most important passages in all of the Old Testament is Ezekiel 20. Notice what the prophet Ezekiel said as he looked into the distant future: "And I will bring you out from the people, and will gather you out of the countries wherein you are scattered, with a mighty hand, and with a stretched out arm, and with fury poured out" (verse 34). God is saying, "I will do it powerfully. I will do it dramatically." Verse 35 adds, "And I will bring you into the wilderness of the people, and there will I plead with you face to face."

Why is God going to plead with His own people face-to-face? Because He is concerned about their heart, their attitude, and their relationship to Him. Verse 38 notes, "And I will purge out from among you the rebels, and them that transgress against me: I will bring them forth out of the country where they sojourn, and they shall not enter into the land of Israel: and ye shall know that I am the LORD." Ezekiel foresees a time when God will come dramatically to spiritually convert the people of Israel and change their heart, soul, and life. The rebels will be purged out.

Then in verse 42 we read, "And ye shall know that I am the LORD, when I shall bring you into the land of Israel, into the country for the which I lifted up mine hand to give it to your fathers." God is saying, "I went out of My way to lift up My hands to give you this nation. It was My promise to Abraham, Isaac, Jacob, their descendants, the descendants of King David, and all those who had a covenant relationship with Me. As you broke the covenant and violated it, you came under My judgment. You were scattered by the Babylonians and by the Romans. I brought you back the first time, but you turned against Me again. I sent the promised Messiah, predicted in the Old Testament, and you did not receive Him. Judgment fell. You have been scattered for 1900 years. And now, for the past 65 years, I have brought you back again into that Promised Land. I am calling on you to understand that My purposes are the most important things in your life. It is not just a matter of national pride and identity. It is a matter of a spiritual heart commitment to Me."

God Himself will provide an opportunity for the people to receive His grace.

> And ye shall loathe yourselves in your own sight for all
> your evils that ye have committed. And ye shall know

> that I am the LORD, when I have wrought with you for
> my name's sake, not according to your wicked ways, nor
> according to your corrupt doings, O ye house of Israel,
> saith the Lord GOD (verses 43-44).

To those who will respond to the grace of God, He says, "I will be your Lord. I will be your God. I will save you. I will cleanse you. I will change you. I will not deal with you according to your past failures. I will deal with you by giving you a new heart and a new spirit and then by making a new covenant, a new agreement with you."

Jesus, who Himself was Jewish, dared to say at His Last Supper, "This cup is the new testament [covenant] in my blood, which is shed for you." If Jesus had been merely a Jewish rabbi, He could not have atoned for His own sins, let alone atone for the sins of others. But He was the Son of God, God incarnate in human flesh. He is the fulfillment of the Old Testament prophecies that promised that God would come to His people. That comes right out of Isaiah 40:3-5. How else could God literally come to us but in human flesh? Jesus is God in sandals. He walks among us, lives above us, and points us to the way of salvation.

This is the whole message of the Old Testament—that the coming Messiah would eventually die. He would be killed and cut off. Isaiah said it (chapter 53), and Daniel said it (chapter 9). How could the Messiah be killed but then reign and rule unless He was resurrected? And how could He be resurrected unless He is the divine Son of God Himself?

It is no mere human being who is going to establish the greatness of Israel in the future. No, it is the Son of God Himself. That is why Jesus came. He came to be the Savior, the banner for Jews and Gentiles alike, to call all of us to faith in the Lord God of the Bible, the God Jehovah, the Creator God who made us in His own image and likeness, so that we might have a relationship with Him.

9

THE MIDDLE EAST CRISIS

The second prophetic sign of the future is a Middle East crisis in the end times. Eventually, the nations of the world will deal with Jerusalem as a "cup of trembling" and a "burdensome stone" (Zechariah 12:2-3)—an international issue that will result in the nations of the Gentiles attacking Jerusalem in the last days. Ezekiel 38–39 describes a war in the Middle East involving the nations that surround Israel from as far north as southern Russia, as far east as Iran, as far west as Libya, and as far south as Sudan. All of those nations will come together in the last days, at the time of the end, and attack the nation and people of Israel.

That invasion has not yet occurred, but as we watch the news or read the headlines each day, we realize that the attitude in the Middle East is often violently opposed to Israel. Islamic extremists and terrorists believe Israel must be destroyed at all costs. There is no willingness to coexist peacefully.

How It All Began

To better understand the nature of this end-time crisis, it is important to recognize the history of the conflict between Israel and its neighbors.[1] The biblical account of the history of both Jews and Arabs is linked to a common source—Abraham. Judaism, Islam, and Christianity are often referred to as the Abrahamic faiths. All three of these religions are founded in one way or another on their connection to Abraham.

Known originally as Abram ("father"), he was called by God to leave ancient Ur and set out for the land of Canaan, which God promised to give to him and his descendants (Genesis 12:1-3). However, after ten years' residence in Canaan, Abram remained childless and became concerned about a successor. So he proposed adopting his chief steward Eliezer of Damascus, an Aramaean, as his heir (Genesis 15:1-2). But God assured him that he would have a son of his own as his heir (verse 4). In response to God's promise, Abram believed and was accounted righteous by God (verse 6). Abram's faith response was so significant that it is recorded five times in the New Testament as the ultimate example of faith in God (Romans 4:3,9,22; Galatians 3:6; James 2:23).

By the end of the day, God literally cut a covenant with Abram, promising to give the land of Canaan to his descendants (Genesis 15:18). However, when Abram tried to explain this to his wife Sarai, she suggested they have the child by a surrogate mother—Hagar, her Egyptian handmaid (Genesis 16:1-3). This was common practice in the ancient Middle East, but it was not what God originally intended. Sarai assumed she was too old to get pregnant, and this was a way of helping God keep His promise. "After all," she may have thought, "what could go wrong?"

Hagar eventually became pregnant with Ishmael, the father of the Arabs (Genesis 16:11-16). Thirteen years of silence separate Genesis 16 and Genesis 17. It is as though God were indicating His disapproval with Abram's actions.

Clearly, God meant for Abram to have the son of promise by his wife Sarai. But we must also observe that none of their actions can be blamed on Ishmael. In fact, God went out of His way twice to spare Ishmael's life (Genesis 16:9-13; 21:9-21). God could have easily solved the Arab-Israeli crisis 4000 years ago by letting Ishmael and Hagar die in the desert. But He did not. Instead, He allowed Ishmael to live and promised to bless him greatly. Ishmael's descendants, the Arab peoples, have just as much opportunity to experience God's grace and salvation as any other people.

The God of the Bible offers the gift of eternal life to whoever believes in the atoning sacrifice of His Son, Jesus Christ (John 3:16). From God's perspective, the problem in the Middle East today is religious, not ethnic. Many Arabs are Christian believers who love the Savior deeply. The real conflict is caused by religious extremists who target all other religions as the enemies of God.

God spares Ishmael's life and promises, "I will make him a great nation" (Genesis 21:18). But He reaffirms His covenant with Abram, changing his name to Abraham ("father of a multitude") and emphasizing that the land of Canaan is promised to his descendants through Isaac, the son of Sarah (Genesis 17:1-21). As we read the entire account of the patriarch and his journey of faith, it becomes obvious that God deliberately waited to allow Sarah to conceive a son in her old age, even after menopause, so the Jewish race would begin with a miraculous conception. Then, 2000 years later, God would intervene in human history with an even greater miracle— the virginal conception of Jesus Christ, the incarnate Son of God (Matthew 1:18-25).

The Old Testament focuses on God's covenantal promises to Israel, the nation that descended from Abraham through Isaac and Jacob. But the Hebrew Scriptures also frequently refer to God's love and grace toward Gentiles (non-Jews). Ruth, a Moabite, is converted to Jehovah and becomes the great-grandmother of David— Israel's greatest King (Ruth 1–4). Joseph marries an Egyptian, Asenath, who becomes the mother of two of the tribes of Israel— Ephraim and Manasseh (Genesis 41:45-52). While dedicating the Jewish temple, Solomon prays that God will hear the prayers of a foreigner, who is not of the people of Israel (1 Kings 8:41). The prophet Isaiah describes the temple as a "house of prayer for all people" (Isaiah 56:7), and he predicts God's light and glory will shine on the Gentiles (Isaiah 62:1-2).

This is the story of two mothers (Hagar and Sarah) and two brothers (Ishmael and Isaac). It is the story of a choice made in human history that now affects human destiny. It is a story that reminds all of us that our choices often have consequences that outlive us. For the Jews, it is a story of a promised destiny that is particular to a promised land—the land of Israel.

Israel's History

The Old Testament opens with the stories of the patriarchs (Abraham, Isaac, and Jacob), who received and believed the promises of God. Next it moves to the period of the exodus from Egypt under Moses's leadership. Then, on to the conquest of the Promised Land by Joshua and its settlement in the days of the judges. Finally, the Hebrew Scriptures take us to the era of the theocratic kingdom—a literal kingdom of God on earth administered by human rulers under the authority of God. But the failure of those rulers eventually led to the collapse of Judah and the fall of Jerusalem to Nebuchadnezzar and the Babylonians in 586 BC.[2]

From that point until the end of the Old Testament record, Israel's future was dominated by the Babylonians (ancient Iraq) and the Persians (ancient Iran). During the Persian period, Cyrus the Great decreed that the Jews could return from the Babylonian captivity to rebuild their temple and their future. Thus the Old Testament closes with the Jews benefiting from Persian benevolence.

Between the Old and New Testaments, the Greeks and then the Romans dominated the Middle East, including Israel, which was divided into various provinces—Judea, Samaria, and Galilee.[3]

As the New Testament opens, Rome is ruling the world. Christianity will be established within its hostile boundaries. In fact, Jesus is executed in a Roman crucifixion sanctioned by Pontius Pilate. After the resurrection of Christ, the disciples received the Great Commission (Matthew 28:19-20) and were empowered on the Feast of Pentecost to carry it out (Acts 2). In the rest of the New Testament, the church is distinct from national Israel. Various Jewish questions remained (including dietary laws, eating with Gentiles, social obligations, and religious practices), but the New Testament church clearly established an identity of its own.

By the end of the New Testament (the apostolic era), the burgeoning young church included more Gentiles than Jews. Peter and Paul were both executed in Rome. John was later exiled to the island of Patmos, where he received the Revelation (Greek, *Apocalypsis*) as the final book of inspired Scripture. From that point onward, Christianity continued to spread beyond the borders of Israel into Europe, Asia, and Africa. In the meantime, Jewish nationalism reached a fervency that led to a rebellion against the Roman Empire. The result was the destruction of Jerusalem in AD 70.

Destruction of the temple (AD 70). Just as Jesus had predicted four decades earlier, the Jewish temple was destroyed by the Romans. The Roman general Titus had earlier besieged the city following a Jewish revolt in AD 66. The result was a Jewish death toll between 500,000 and one million. Many Christian Jews in Jerusalem probably escaped because Jesus had predicted the impending destruction in his Olivet Discourse (Luke 21:5-24).

The Christian Jews had watched as Vespasian and his Roman army surrounded Jerusalem two years earlier in AD 68. But before he could lay siege to the city, Vespasian broke off the attack and returned to Rome in order to claim the throne. Vespasian then turned control of the Roman army over to his son Titus, who returned to Jerusalem in AD 70 and proceeded to destroy the city and Herod's temple. The Christian Jews likely heeded Jesus's prophecy and fled the city ahead of time.

The Bar Kochba rebellion (AD 135). Following Emperor Hadrian's announcement that he was going to build a pagan temple on the site of the temple ruins and restrict the practice of the Jewish religion, another Jewish rebellion arose in Jerusalem led by Simon Bar Kochba. More than half a million were killed during the fighting, and the Bar Kochba revolt failed, resulting in the almost total expulsion of Jews from their ancient homeland.

The Roman period (AD 135–640). Under the direction of the Roman government, a new city called Aelia Capitolina was built over the ruins of Jerusalem. Jews were forbidden to set foot inside the new city under penalty of death. A pagan temple was also constructed, and the name of the province of Judah was changed to Syria Palestina, from which the name Palestine was later derived.

In AD 325, the Roman emperor Constantine was converted to Christianity, and the Roman Empire eventually became Christianized. During the period known as the Byzantine Empire (AD 325–640), Christianity was the dominant religion in Europe, the Middle East, and North Africa. The emperors continued to rule from Constantinople, but they lost control of the entire Middle East to the sweeping effects of the Muslim conquest in the seventh century.[4]

The Rule of Islam

The Muslim period (640–1090). Not long after the death of Muhammad, his Muslim followers conquered Palestine, and contact with the West was virtually cut off. During this period, the Mosque of Omar (Dome of the Rock) and the Al-Aqsa Mosque were built on the Temple Mount, where they have now stood for nearly 1300 years as symbols of Muslim domination. To this very day, the Islamic control of the Temple Mount has prevented the Jews from rebuilding their own temple on this holy site.

Latin or Crusader period (1099–1291). During this stormy period, European Christian Crusaders invaded the Holy Land in an attempt to take it back from the Muslims, who had recently desecrated some ancient Christian sites, including the Tomb of the Holy Sepulcher. Both Muslims and Jews were slaughtered as a result of the First Crusade when the overzealous crusaders took Jerusalem and established it as the Latin kingdom of Jerusalem under the auspices of the Roman church. Many today forget that the city was Christianized for more than 100 years and that other parts of Palestine remained under European control for nearly 200 years until the last Crusader fortress fell.

Saladin and the Mamluks (1187–1517). The Syrian Muslim scholar Ali ibn Tahir al-Sulami revived the idea of calling for *jihad* ("holy war") to recapture the holy city from the Crusaders. In response, Saladin rallied 30,000 soldiers in Syria, crossed the Jordan, and overwhelmingly defeated the Crusader force of 20,000 at the Horns of Hittim in Galilee on June 30, 1187. By October 2, Jerusalem surrendered to Saladin after a two-week siege. In the aftermath, the Muslims made a determined effort to re-Islamize Jerusalem. The golden cross of the Crusaders was removed from the Al-Aqsa Mosque, and the Roman altar was removed from the Dome of the Rock. However, in the years that followed there were continual conflicts between Muslims and Crusaders. In 1219, Saladin's nephew, al-Mu'azzam, ordered the destruction of Jerusalem's walls and depopulated the city to keep it from the Crusaders. By 1260, the city came under the control of the Mamluks.

Ottoman Turkish period (1517–1917). The Mamluks were replaced by the Turks in 1517. Jerusalem was rebuilt as a Turkish Muslim city by Sulayman the Magnificent (1520–1556). During this time, the Islamic influence on the culture of Palestine continued to grow. The rebuilding of Jerusalem's walls was completed in 1566, and they still stand today, enclosing the Old City. Despite numerous local conflicts, the Turkish period provided general protection from foreign invasions and ultimately opened contact with the Western world during the nineteenth century. However, the fate of Israel changed dramatically during World War I when the Turks allied themselves with Kaiser Wilhelm of Germany. Germany lost the war, and the Turks lost control of Palestine to the British, who set up a mandate over the region from 1917 to 1948.

Modern History of Israel and Its Neighbors

The Zionist movement. Curiously, the Jews' interest in returning to the Holy Land was sparked not only by various Jewish movements but also by nineteenth-century Christians. Western

Christians' increasing attention to the second coming of Christ revived thoughts about the Jews returning to their homeland as a sign of the end times. Prophetic literature and debates on the subject began to materialize, which in turn influenced sermons and missionary visions of churches in the West. Not surprisingly, this movement coincided with the revival of the literal interpretation of prophetic Scripture in the church. This in turn sparked interest among many displaced and homeless Jews for an Israeli homeland. Simultaneously, Baron Edmond de Rothschild launched a program of agricultural colonies in Palestine that were profitable to European Jews.

The Society for Colonizing Palestine formed in London in 1861. This organization and similar groups throughout Europe eventually helped to popularize the idea of Jewish emigration to Israel. But it didn't happen overnight. Faithful Jewish believers met regularly in their synagogues to read God's promises to Israel recorded in Deuteronomy and other Old Testament passages. They collectively began to pray a prayer that would define their destiny in the decades to come: "Next year in Jerusalem."

Through God's providence, an adverse event that occurred in France in 1894 would be transformed into an opportunity for the Jews. Captain Alfred Dreyfus, a French Jew and an exceptional army officer, was made the scapegoat for a serious military scandal. He was disgraced and sentenced to Devil's Island as a criminal. Only after several years was his innocence firmly established. This incident drew worldwide attention in the media and reaffirmed on a global scale that Jews were not immune from anti-Semitism and persecution. They concluded that having their own sovereign state and national homeland would be the only means by which they could be kept safe from the kind of discrimination that had followed them for the past 1900 years.

Austrian journalist Theodor Herzl was impressed by the Dreyfus affair, which he had written about for his newspaper in 1894. He subsequently convened the First Zionist Congress in Basel, Switzerland, three years later. Jewish leaders from most of the Western countries attended. The Congress quickly adopted a resolution that read, "Zionism strives to create for the Jewish people a home in Palestine secured by public law." By 1914, Palestine had more than 75,000 resident Jews and more than 40 agricultural settlements.[5]

British rule begins. In 1917, Arthur Balfour, foreign secretary of Great Britain, issued the Balfour Declaration, which laid the groundwork for the eventual British mandate over Palestine, which was legally granted by the League of Nations as a homeland for the Jewish people. The United Kingdom's disciplined presence in that tumultuous region ultimately kept the Arabs from driving the defenseless and outnumbered Jews into the sea.

By 1939, with constant unrest in Palestine, Great Britain began to go back on the Balfour Declaration and instead favor Arab independence and control of the area. Nevertheless, Jewish immigration continued, accelerated by intense persecution under the Nazi regime before and during World War II. By the time Great Britain relinquished control of the region in 1947, some 670,000 Jews inhabited the land and were able to defend themselves.

The Foundation of the Middle East Crisis

Although the Jewish–Arab conflict can be traced all the way back to the time of Abraham, the clash would take on greater significance as the prospect of Israel gaining statehood began to gain momentum.

1939—Emigration of Jews from Europe increased as Hitler built a network of concentration camps. By the end of World War II, six million Jews had died at the hands of the Nazis and Russian communists. Thousands of Jews fled to Palestine for refuge.

November 2, 1943—Lebanon gained independence from France. Two months later, France relinquished its mandate powers over

Syria, which led to Syria's establishment as an independent nation. European influence in the Middle East began to diminish.

March 22, 1945—The Arab league united Egypt, Syria, Lebanon, Iraq, Saudi Arabia, Yemen, and Transjordan. This was the first move toward unity among Arabs, who shared an intense opposition to the establishment of a Jewish state.

May 7, 1945—With the collapse of Germany at the end of World War II, the Allies liberated Jewish prisoners from Auschwitz, Dachau, and other concentration camps. Worldwide shock and sympathy along with Jewish wealth from around the world encouraged the relocation of more than a million displaced Jews to Palestine. The process of assimilation began and further inflamed the Arabs.

November 29, 1947—The United Nations voted to partition Palestine into two states, Jewish and Arab. Jerusalem was declared an international city, open to all as the holy city of Jews, Catholics, Protestants, and Muslims. Although the Jews accepted the plan, the Arabs wanted no part of it. Fearing a civil war, 300,000 Palestinian Arabs fled the country.

May 14, 1948—The United Nations officially recognized the State of Israel. US president Harry Truman determined the deciding vote. The Israeli government established the State of Israel, fulfilling the 2500-year-old prophecy recorded in Ezekiel 37. Great Britain ended its mandate in Palestine and removed its troops, leaving behind more than 650,000 Jews to govern themselves. This turn of events was unacceptable to the Arab world. Within hours of the declaration of sovereignty, Egypt, Syria, Saudi Arabia, Lebanon, Iraq, and Transjordan declared war on Israel. The Arab armies easily outnumbered the Israelis, and although thousands of Jews died in the ensuing combat, Israel miraculously defeated its Arab neighbors. Some 350,000 additional Arabs who refused to recognize the State of Israel fled to neighboring Arab countries such as Lebanon, Syria, Transjordan, Iraq, and Saudi Arabia.

1956—Egypt, under the direction of Colonel Gamel Abdel Nassar, tried to nationalize the Suez Canal following British withdrawal from the area. Israel invaded the Sinai Peninsula and in eight days reached the canal, gaining control over the northernmost point of the Gulf of Aqaba. Nassar suffered a military defeat but gained an eventual political victory by retaining control of the Suez Canal.

1964—The Palestine Liberation organization (PLO) was founded by Palestinian refugees in order to create an armed force capable of coercing Israel to give up land that could be used for an independent Arab-controlled Palestine. The move led to inflamed Palestinian nationalism that would result in a series of wars and conflicts that continue until this day.

1967—The Six-Day War. The Israeli intelligence agency, Mossad, uncovered Arab plans to launch an immediate military attack against Israel. Mossad also discovered that Russia was in the process of supplying large shipments of arms to these same Arab countries. Rather than waiting for the Arab assault, Israel launched predawn land and air strikes against Egypt, Jordan, and Syria. Although outnumbered 30 to 1, Israel was nevertheless able to quickly destroy the Egyptian air force and navy as well as overcome Syria from the air. Israel's tanks reached the Suez Canal and decisively captured Soviet-built missile bases intact.

The war lasted less than a week—hence the name Six-Day War. With its stunning military victory, Israel controlled the Sinai Peninsula, the West Bank, and the Golan Heights. This more than quadrupled Israel's territory from 8000 to 34,000 square miles. For the first time since the Roman era, the city of Jerusalem was under Jewish control. However, within a few days of the victory, Israeli Defense Minister Moshe Dayan, meeting with Muslim leaders at the Al-Aqsa Mosque, returned administrative control of the Temple Mount site over to the Palestinians, declaring Jerusalem to be an international city.

1973—Syria and Egypt attacked Israel while Jews were in their synagogues observing Yom Kippur, the Day of Atonement. The three-week-long Yom Kippur War began. This was the only time the Israeli military was caught unprepared for an attack. Once again, the Arabs, equipped with Russian armament, attacked Israel in simultaneous operations. Egypt seized large portions of the Sinai, and Syria took the Golan Heights. Israel, however, was able to break through enemy lines and cross the Suez Canal, thereby cutting off the advancing Egyptian army. At the same time, Israel retook the Golan Heights, forged into Syria, and was poised to conquer Damascus but stopped when the UN enforced a cease-fire. Israel won this war as well but suffered tremendous casualties.

1978—At a conference hosted by US president Jimmy Carter at Camp David in Maryland, President Anwar Sadat of Egypt and Prime Minister Menachem Begin of Israel signed agreements known as the Camp David Accords. This event led to the signing of a formal peace treaty between the two countries on March 26, 1979. In keeping with this agreement, Israel officially withdrew its troops from the city of El Arish and returned the Sinai to Egyptian control.

1981—In a daring early-morning raid, 14 Israeli F-16s and F-15s flew 600 miles north of their air base and destroyed the French-built nuclear generator in Baghdad, Iraq. Israel believed that Iraq was planning to utilize the plutonium generator to build atomic weapons for use against Israel. The world was outraged by Israel's actions, but many world leaders were secretly relieved that the hostile and unpredictable Iraq would not become a nuclear power.

1981—President Sadat of Egypt was assassinated on October 6 while watching a military parade. The incident was traced to Arab terrorists opposed to Sadat's friendly attitude toward Israel. Hosni Mubarak, Sadat's successor, subsequently opened Egypt's borders to Libya but maintained the official peace treaty with Israel.

1983—A truck bomb blew up the US Marine Compound at the Beirut, Lebanon, airport, killing 240 marines, who were part of a peace-keeping force. A similar attack at the French compound killed an additional 56 soldiers, shattering confidence in a lasting peace in the region.

1984—Eight thousand Jews were secretly rescued from Ethiopia and brought safely to Israel as part of an effort called Operation Moses. During the 1980s and 1990s, thousands of Jews were brought to Israel from Iraq, Iran, and the nations of the former Soviet Union.

1987—On December 6, an Israeli was stabbed to death while shopping in Gaza. The next day, four residents of the Jabalya refugee camp in Gaza were killed in a traffic accident. Rumors began spreading among the Palestinians that the four accident victims had been killed by Israelis out of revenge. Mass rioting broke out two days later and spread across the West Bank, Gaza, and Jerusalem in what would become known as the First Intifada. The violence, orchestrated by the PLO and directed toward Israeli soldiers and civilians, continued for the next four years. During this time 27 Israelis were killed and more than 3100 injured.

1990—On August 2, Saddam Hussein of Iraq invaded Kuwait. Four days later, the UN Security Council imposed economic sanctions against Iraq. The next day, the United States began sending troops into the Persian Gulf area. Hussein announced that any military action taken against Iraq would result in a strike on Israel. Iraqi Foreign Minister Tariq Aziz threatened that Iraq would use chemical weapons if Israel decided to strike back. On December 23, Saddam Hussein announced that Tel Aviv would be Iraq's first target if invaded.

1991—The Gulf War began on January 15. Over the next five weeks, Iraq launched 38 Scud missiles at Israel, resulting in one fatality and 172 injuries. On February 28, the Gulf War ended with the expulsion of the Iraqi army from Kuwait by US and coalition forces.

1993—Israel secretly signed a peace agreement with the PLO in Oslo, Norway, on August 20. Several days later, both groups formally recognized each other's right to exist. On September 13, the historic handshake took place between Israel's prime minister Yitzhak Rabin and PLO leader Yasser Arafat. On September 23, the Israeli Knesset (legislature) ratified the Oslo Agreement by a vote of 61 to 50. One year later Rabin and Arafat were awarded the Nobel Peace Prize.

1995—Israeli prime minister Yitzhak Rabin was assassinated at a peace rally by a Jewish extremist. Heads of state from all over the world, including Jordan's King Hussein and President Mubarak of Egypt, attended Rabin's funeral in Jerusalem. Yigal Amir was later indicted for the murder. The future of the Israeli–PLO negotiations were now in doubt.

1996—Jerusalem celebrated its 3000-year anniversary as the capital of the Jewish state, dating back to King David's conquest of the city in biblical times. Later that year, newly elected Israeli prime minister Benjamin Netanyahu announced the opening of a new archaeological tunnel alongside the Western Wall in Jerusalem, triggering a deadly series of Palestinian protests that resulted in 14 Israeli and 56 Palestinian deaths.

1998—The US embassies in Nairobi, Kenya, and Tanzania were simultaneously bombed by Al-Qaeda terrorists, resulting in 257 dead and more than 4000 wounded. Islamic terrorist leader Osama bin Laden was later confirmed to be the mastermind behind the massacre. The Israeli Defense Force aided in the rescue efforts in Nairobi. Later that same year, at the urging of US president Bill

Clinton and King Hussein of Jordan, Netanyahu and Arafat signed the Wye River Memorandum to redeploy portions of the West Bank and Gaza Strip to the Palestinian Authority.

2000—US president Bill Clinton attempted to negotiate a peace treaty between Israeli prime minister Ehud Barak and Palestinian president Yasser Arafat. Barak agreed but Arafat refused. Immediately thereafter the Second Intifada (Muslim resistance) began with numerous suicide bombings of civilians in Israel.

September 11, 2001—Islamic terrorists sponsored by Al Qaeda hijacked and crashed jetliners into the World Trade Center in New York and the Pentagon in Washington, DC. Nearly 3000 people were killed. Thousands of Palestinians and other Muslims celebrated in the streets while the rest of the world mourned and expressed outrage. The United States retaliated by invading Al Qaeda–dominated Afghanistan, setting up a democratically elected government in the Islamic nation and eventually executing Osama bin Laden, who masterminded the attack.

2002—Israel erected a security fence (wall) along the West Bank to help prevent future terrorist infiltrations into Israel. On October 16, Israeli prime minister Ariel Sharon met with US president George W. Bush, who proposed a peace plan known as the Road Map, which called for the creation of a permanent Palestinian state.

2005—Mahmoud Abbas, chairman of the Palestine Liberation Organization, was elected the new president of the Palestinian National Authority, replacing Yasser Arafat, who had died two months earlier in Paris. Early in 2006, Ariel Sharon suffered a severe stroke and was replaced by Ehud Olmert.

2006—After a series of air and missile attacks between Israel and Hezbollah in Lebanon, Iranian president Mahmoud Ahmadinejad announced that "Israel will one day be wiped out just as the Soviet

Union was," drawing applause from participants in a Holocaust-denying rally in Tehran.

2011–2013 —The so-called Arab Spring included the overthrow of the governments of Tunisia, Libya, and Egypt and a civil war in Syria, resulting in the loss of thousands of lives.

2013—Ahmadinejad was replaced by Hassan Rouhani, who called for more peaceful relations with the West in order to renew Iran's efforts to gain nuclear power, despite public protests from Islamic extremists in Iran and warnings against his sincerity from the Israelis.

We can readily see from this list of significant events that the modern state of Israel is in a unique and precarious position in history. God is obviously doing something unusual in our times.

History indicates that onlookers in the Western world should not assume that people in the Middle East will resolve their conflicts peacefully. According to the Bible, it will not happen! That is why we are so committed to defend the cause of the people and nation of Israel. For the most part, the Jewish people have not yet come to belief in the Messiah. But the Word of God makes it clear that whoever blesses the sons of Abraham will be blessed, and whoever curses them will be cursed (Genesis 12:3). God has blessed America uniquely over the years because of its special relationship with and support of Israel.

However, if our nation moves away from Israel, we would leave them vulnerable. We also leave ourselves vulnerable to the judgment of God, and we leave our future, from a human standpoint, up for grabs. Yet God is still on the throne. He knows what He is doing. In the end, the crisis in the Middle East will be resolved by God Himself.

10

A GLOBAL ECONOMY

A third sign that reveals the future seemed almost impossible to fulfill for many centuries—the prophecy of the global economy in the last days. Yet today, the majority of transactions in many developed nations are digital, taking place with credit cards or online banking. Mobile banking has also become the norm in many developing nations, allowing anyone with a smartphone or tablet to conduct business in a cashless society.

This is a reality in the day and age in which we live. What happens in the stock market in China affects the stock market in Europe, which affects the stock market in America, and the cycle goes on and on around the globe.

In Revelation 13, we read the amazing prophecy about the mark of the beast. The Scripture says that the false prophet, the false religious leader who assists the Antichrist, will cause everybody "both small and great, rich and poor, free and bond, to receive a mark in their right hand, or in their foreheads" (verse 16).

What is the role of this global economy in the end times? Dr. Thomas Ice explains the relationship between global government and the coming global economy.

> The Bible teaches that during the seven-year tribulation there will be a global government for at least the final three and a half years. Revelation 17–18 indicates that the Babylonian globalization will be built upon three major planks: economic trade, false religion, and centralized

government. Obviously we do not yet live in the time of the coming seven-year tribulation. But we do live in a time where God is setting the stage for events that will take place after the rapture, during the tribulation. Globalization is one of those things that will characterize the tribulation. We are seeing it take place daily, all around us. Everywhere you look institutions, whether private or public, are moving toward globalism.[1]

The future holds not only a one-world alliance of governing powers but also a single, united financial system. Bible readers often speculate about one important aspect of this system—the mark of the beast.

The Meaning of the Mark

The Greek word translated *mark* is *charagma*. It refers to a tattoo but could include any kind of mark. Each of the seven instances of the word for *mark* or *sign* in the Greek New Testament appears in Revelation and refers to the mark of the beast (Revelation 13:16-17; 14:9,11; 16:2; 19:20; 20:4). Technology already allows a simple electronic chip to be inserted under the skin. Any variation could fit this prediction.

Then the text says that no person could buy or sell unless he or she had one of three things: the mark of the beast, the name of the beast, or the number of the beast (Revelation 13:17). The mark, or insignia, identifies the name and number of the beast. The chapter concludes, "Here is wisdom. Let him that hath understanding count the number of the beast: for it is the number of a man; and his number is Six hundred threescore and six" (verse 18).

It is not just three sixes. It has to add up to 666. You can debate forever what it is, when it is, and how it is. But the point is, this insignia is used to control the global economy. Look at a typical credit card—what does it have on it? It has a name, it has a number, and it has an insignia. We already have the devices in place for controlling a global economy.

The Bible explains that the mark will be...

- the Antichrist's mark, identified with his person
- the actual number 666, not a representation
- a mark, like a tattoo
- visible to the naked eye
- on people, not in them
- recognized, not questioned
- voluntary, not involuntary or given through deception
- used after the rapture, not before
- used in the second half of the tribulation
- needed to buy and sell
- received by all non-Christians but rejected by all Christians
- a sign of worship and allegiance to the Antichrist
- promoted by the false prophet

The destiny of all who receive the mark will be eternal punishment in the lake of fire.[2]

How all of these things will ultimately work out is up to God. The people who will devise these things will think they are providing convenient ways to transact business. However, the Bible warns us that when the global economy becomes a reality, an evil world leader will eventually control it.

The Purpose of the Mark

The purpose of the mark will be to control financial transactions. Young people find this perspective difficult to fathom, but it is not without historical precedent, as Dr. LaHaye reminds us.

This economic pressure will be instrumental in causing many weak, worldly individuals to succumb to the establishment of this monarch, which will be tantamount to the personal rejection of Christ and acceptance of Antichrist. One can scarcely imagine the pressures of having to possess such a mark in order to secure the necessary food for his family. The U.S. government in World War II furnished a device of this kind in the form of food rationing. It was not enough to have money sufficient to pay for an item, for one had to have food stamps. The same will be true during the second half of the tribulation, for the Antichrist will so control the economy that no one can live if he or she does not worship him.[3]

Those who refuse the mark will be unable to buy or sell, leaving only alternative, underground systems for obtaining food or bartering goods. People will continue to come to faith in Jesus Christ during this time, but they will do so at great cost.

What About the United States?

Today, the US dollar remains the standard of currency across much of the world. Yet the Bible predicts a time when a new world order will exist and a new type of currency will become the standard. Do we see any hints now that such changes are already beginning to take place? Dr. Thomas Ice commented on this in an article for the Pre-Trib Research Center.

Previously, the United States was often the one standing in the way of a global economy and government. We are not yet there for either, but who can doubt that since the beginning of the Obama presidency that we are indeed seeing change and moving into harmony with the one world government crowd. In the past the United States stood in the way and acted in her national interest, as I believe we should still do, but now we are the last domino to fall and nothing of significance appears to stand in the way of globalism. Only the future return of Christ after the tribulation will really bring change for Christians.[4]

The United States and its economy continue to influence the world, but the shifting tides could quickly cause the nations of the world to accept a new global monetary system under a future Antichrist. What seemed impossible only a few years ago now continues to take shape as God's ultimate fulfillment of prophecy unfolds. Prophecy scholar Mark Hitchcock adds this:

> The Bible clearly links the global mark of the beast system with the emergence of a cashless society…While no one on earth knows what the final fallout will be from the world economic crisis, it's clear that the world is ripe for a universal economic strategy and a charismatic leader to bring the world together.[5]

Seven Future Players in the Global Economy

Revelation 12–13 lists the seven symbolic players in the great end-times drama. As we learn who they are and what significant roles they will have in the final days of world history, we can understand better where we are in relation to God's ultimate plan and purpose.

The Bible reminds us that even though we sense the end is near, it will not necessarily happen tomorrow. In fact, the world will not be plunged into Armageddon, the final conflict, until after a whole series of events takes place. The Lord has to come back and rapture the church home to heaven. Then during the time of tribulation, seven symbolic players must all come to the forefront in unique ways before the church triumphant returns with Christ. Let's take a look at who these players are, what they are, and what they mean to the future of the world.

The Woman

We first meet a unique woman. "And there appeared a great wonder in heaven; a woman clothed with the sun, and the moon under her feet, and upon her head a crown of twelve stars" (Revelation 12:1).

Here John, as he writes the Revelation, is using symbolism from Joseph's dream about himself and his family members, who were represented by the sun, the moon, and the stars (Genesis 37:9-10). Every Jewish person reading this passage during the first century would have understood immediately that the woman symbolizes the nation of Israel.

Revelation 12:2 explains, "And she, being with child cried, travailing in birth, and pained to be delivered." The woman is in turmoil, about to deliver a baby. There has been great speculation throughout church history about the woman's identity. Some have said it refers to Mary, the mother of Jesus. Others have said this is the church because the woman is persecuted and has to flee for her life. But when we look at the entire Bible, it becomes obvious that the woman is a symbol of the nation and people of Israel. Israel is, in essence, the mother of Christ. This is certainly not the church. The church is the bride of Christ. The woman here is the mother of Christ. He is the male child who is going to be delivered into the world, and Satan is going to attempt to destroy Him.

Four women play unique roles in the book of Revelation:

- the persecuted woman—Israel (chapter 12)
- the bloody harlot—the false church (chapter 17)
- the arrogant queen—the political system of the Antichrist (chapter 18)
- the pure bride—the true church, the bride of Christ (chapter 19)

The woman in chapter 12 is not the bride. She is the mother. She is not the church. This is Israel. Jesus is a descendant of the line of

Abraham, Isaac, and Jacob. Jesus is a Jewish Savior who came to the Jewish people to offer Himself as the King. But when the nation rejected Him, He said to the disciples, "Go ye therefore, and teach *all nations*, baptizing them in the name of the Father, and of the Son, and of the Holy Spirit" (Matthew 28:18-20).

The message of the gospel is the message of the death, burial, and resurrection of Christ. It is a message designed to change the world. And as the world responds in faith to Christ, the true church—not a particular denomination, but the true believers who know Jesus Christ as their personal Savior—will one day be caught away in the rapture. But in the time of tribulation that follows, the seven significant players come to the forefront.

The first of those significant players is Israel. It has often been said, "If you want to know where we are in the timetable of God, as we look at the final signs of the future, keep your eye on the nation and people of Israel." God dealt with the people of Israel for the centuries of the Old Testament. Then, with the beginning of the church age, He turned His attention to the church. But after the rapture of the church, God's attention again will be focused on the nation and people of Israel. The two witnesses will arise from among them in the spirit of Moses and Elijah (Revelation 11). The 144,000 will arise from among them to proclaim the message of Christ in the time of tribulation (Revelation 7:4-8).

God has not abandoned His people Israel. God still has a plan and a purpose for them. But it will take the dramatic experience of the rapture to convince them that they indeed have been left behind and that they will become significant players in the end-times drama as the focus of biblical prophecy again resides on the nation and people of Israel.

The Dragon

We have seen that the first symbol is the woman, the mother of Christ, the nation and people of Israel. Jesus descends through the line of the Jews and comes to bring salvation through them. Then we see the second symbol: "And there appeared another wonder in heaven; and, behold a great red dragon, having seven heads and ten horns, and seven crowns upon his heads" (Revelation 12:3).

John goes on to tell us in verse 9 that the dragon is the serpent—the devil, or Satan. So there is no debate as to who the red dragon symbolizes in the book of Revelation. It is the symbol of Satan himself. He is the power behind the ungodly world system of the last days. In fact, Satan has been at war with God from the beginning of time. But that war will reach a climax during the time of the tribulation period.

The Male Child

In verse 5, we have a third symbol, a male child: "And she brought forth a man child [literally, a male child] who was to rule all nations with a rod of iron: and her child was caught up unto God, and to his throne." Most Bible commentators agree that this is a reference to Jesus Christ. He is the child who is born. He is the Son of David, the Son of promise, the promised Messiah, the Savior of the world. In His ascension, He returned to the throne of God in heaven. Satan cannot destroy the Messiah in heaven and cannot destroy the raptured church, so he turns his anger and vitriolic attention against the nation and people of Israel in an attempt to destroy them. He pushes them to the brink of destruction, and they finally call on Christ as Savior, Lord, and Messiah.

Michael

The fourth symbol in the passage is Michael the archangel. "And there was war in heaven: Michael and his angels fought against the dragon; and the dragon fought and his angels, and prevailed not; neither was their place found any more in heaven" (Revelation 12:7-8).

They were cast out. Some people read this and ask, "Didn't this happen in eternity past, when Satan fell the first time?" The answer is no. Satan fell from his position as Lucifer, the covering cherub, the shining one, in eternity past. But Satan still has access to the presence of God. In the book of Job, he still comes with the sons of God, the angels, to give a report to God, and he argues with God about why He has blessed Job so much (Job 1:6; 2:1). Satan had access to heaven during the events recorded in the book of Job. He had not been permanently kicked out. Notice what Revelation 12:10 says: "And I heard a loud voice saying in heaven, Now is come salvation, and strength, and the kingdom of our God, and the power of his Christ: for the accuser of our brethren is cast down, who accused them before our God day and night."

Throughout the centuries of church history, Satan has continued to go before the throne of God to accuse the brethren, the believers. He still loves to point an accusing finger and say, "Look at him. Look at what he did. Listen to what she said. How in the world can You save them? How can they be Christians?" He constantly accuses the people of God and the things of God and disturbs the stability of the world. He is doing everything he can to fight against the things of God. This passage reveals that this will go on for a long time. Finally God will say, "Enough. Throw him out of here. Cast him to the earth."

How do we know that Revelation 12:10 will be fulfilled in the future and that it doesn't refer to a past event? First, Satan still has access to the presence of God. Second, he is still the accuser of the brethren. He still wanders about, seeking whom he may devour. But verse 12 is clear:

> Therefore rejoice, ye heavens, and ye that dwell in them. Woe to the inhabiters of the earth and of the sea! for the devil is come down unto you, having great wrath, because he knoweth that he hath but a short time.

Satan, having been cast out, has but a short time—certainly not 21 centuries. In verse 13 he is cast to the earth for a short time. Then verse 14 reveals, "And to the woman were given two wings of a great eagle, that she might fly into the wilderness, into her place, where she is nourished for a time, and times, and half a time, from the face of the serpent."

This verse specifies three and a half times, or three and a half years. That makes it clear that Satan will finally be cast out of heaven to the earth, where he has no more access to the presence of God, sometime in the future. And when it happens, he has only three and a half years left to torment the "seed of the woman" during the great tribulation.

The Remnant

The tribulation period lasts seven years according to the book of Daniel. So this event occurs at the midpoint of the tribulation period. Satan is cast out of heaven to the earth. He then turns his persecution against the woman, the people of Israel, and drives her into the wilderness.

Then verse 17 introduces us to the fifth symbol in this passage: "And the dragon was wroth with the woman, and went to make war with the remnant of her seed, which keep the commandments of God, and have the testimony of Jesus Christ." These are the saved Jews of the tribulation period. They flee from Jerusalem into the wilderness until the return of Christ.

The Beast of the Sea

There are two more key players in the end-time drama: the beast and the false prophet. Revelation 13 begins, "And I stood upon the sand of the sea, and saw a beast rise up out of the sea."

Throughout the book of Revelation, John describes the Antichrist as a beast. Elsewhere in the Bible, he is called the man of sin, the son of perdition, the lawless one, the worthless shepherd, and the abomination. But we know him theologically as the *antichristos*, the one who is against Christ, the beast himself. As John describes him, he says of the beast, "And all that dwell upon the earth shall worship him, whose names are not written in the book of life" (verse 8).

In other words, all of the unsaved of the tribulation period, all of those who do not come to faith in Christ, who do not repent, whose names are not written in the book of life, will end up worshipping the beast, following the beast, and being deceived by the beast. That great end-times ruler is described in the Bible as having awe-inspiring intelligence, power, and persuasiveness. He will have political, social, economic, and religious control of the entire world.

The Beast of the Earth

Revelation 13 also introduces us to the seventh symbolic player in the end-times drama, the beast out of the earth, later called the false prophet. "And I beheld another beast coming up out of the earth; and he had two horns like a lamb, and he spake as a dragon" (verse 11).

He appears to be religious. He even looks harmless. But he sounds like the devil himself. Verse 12 adds, "And he exerciseth all the power of the first beast before him, and causeth the earth and them which dwell therein to worship the first beast." The first beast is the Antichrist. The second beast is the false prophet.

> [He] deceiveth them that dwell on the earth by the means of those miracles which he had power to do in the sight of the beast; saying to them that dwell on the earth, that they should make an image to the beast, that had the wound by a sword, and did live. And he had power to give life unto the image of the beast, that the image of the beast should both speak, and cause that as many as would not worship the image of the beast should be killed. And he causeth all, both small and great, rich and poor, free and bond, to receive a mark in their right hand, or in their foreheads: and that no man might buy or sell,

save he that had the mark, or the name of the beast, or
the number of his name (verses 14-17).

When Will the Global Economy Occur?

In 1973, I was on a flight with Delta. I pulled a copy of *Sky* magazine out of the pouch and read an article about the coming cashless
society—and that was 40 years ago! The article said the day would
come when cash would be almost meaningless to people. Everybody would use credit cards and make cashless transactions. Money
would be moved from one account to another automatically. This
was going to be the wave of the future.

The article implied these developments would happen in the
next 5 or 10 years, but they did not. But after 30 to 40 years, they
have become reality. We are living in a day and age unlike anything
the world has ever seen. All of that change causes much concern and
many questions because the Bible clearly predicts that in the end
times, a sinister figure, the Antichrist, will control a global economy.

In his well-documented book *The End of Money*, Mark Hitchcock makes the following eight important observations and appli-
cations regarding the coming cashless society.

- The mark is future, not past.

- The mark is a literal, visible brand, mark, or tattoo that
  will be placed on the right hand or forehead of people
  during the great tribulation.

- The mark will be given as a sign of devotion to the Antichrist and as a passport to engage in commerce.

- The mark will be the number 666, which will be the
  numerical value of the Antichrist's name. This information will enable the saints who are alive at the time of
  the tribulation to "count the number of the beast" and
  identify him.

- Those who take the mark will be eternally doomed.

- Until the rapture has taken place, no one should attempt to identify the Antichrist or his mark—the number 666.

- The latest technological methods of identifying and locating people strikingly foreshadow the Antichrist's ability to control the world, but it is not possible to determine how technology will be employed to fulfill this prophecy. But the technology that's now available certainly makes the implementation of such a system not only possible, but probable.

- In spite of its association with evil, the number 666 will be received by those who willfully reject God.[6]

Today, nations are not living as isolated villages separated from one another. We are a global community whether we like it or not. It is all part of the convenience of a modern society with high-speed travel, computer technology, satellite transmissions, and so on. Even as we proclaim the gospel through the Internet, television, mobile technology, and other means, lives are being changed around the world due to the use of modern technology.

The technology is not evil. It can be used for good. But it can also be used for wrong. It all depends on who is using it and for what purpose. Scripture is telling that in the last days, a time will come when the global economy will be controlled by a world leader. The global nature of today's economy tells us we are closer than we have ever been to the time of the end.

11

THE EUROPEAN UNION

In the 1990s, the nations of Europe officially formed an alliance known as the European Union (EU). It is based on the earlier formations of the European Economic Community (EEC), which was established after World War II. It created the single largest financial market in the world, and many people compared it to the Roman Empire of old. This development marks an eerie connection with the fourth prophetic sign that reveals the future—the unification of the European nations.

The Bible makes it clear that the old Roman Empire will ultimately give rise to a new Roman Empire at the time of the end. Scholars have struggled for years trying to sort out all the details, but certain passages in the Bible seem to make this shift very clear.

For example, in Daniel 9:26, the prophet Daniel is given a glimpse into the distant future. He says a time will come when the Messiah would appear, but He would then be cut off and killed. And "the people of the prince that shall come [the Antichrist, the world ruler] shall destroy the city and the sanctuary [the temple]," and the end will come with a war of desolations.

We know from history that Daniel was being told by the Spirit of God that the Messiah would come and the temple would be rebuilt, but the Messiah eventually would be killed and the temple would be destroyed. All of those things happened. But notice that the people who destroyed the city and the temple are the people from whom the prince will come. That was the ancient Romans.

So the world leader of the last days will come from the new Roman Empire—basically, Europe.

Leaders have tried to unite Europe—Napoleon tried, Hitler tried—but no one has succeeded. But today Europe is coming together to encourage economic cooperation. What was the European Economic Community is now the European Union. As we look at what is happening in our world today, we see that we are closer than we have ever been to the time of the end.

Why Europe?

Much has been written about the empire of the Antichrist. Some believe it will be centered in Babylon (modern Iraq). Others have suggested America as a possibility. But the Bible itself clearly identifies Europe as the final Gentile world power. Americans are quick to ask, where is the United States in Bible prophecy? But the better question is, where is Europe in Bible prophecy?

The United States did not exist when the Bible was written. Therefore, it does not clearly appear in the Bible. One can make a case of America in prophecy only by associating it with Europe. As a nation of predominantly European immigrants, the United States could possibly qualify among the "young lions" of Tarshish (Ezekiel 38:13). The United States could also be included with general references to the revived Roman Empire. Otherwise, prophecy students have to stretch a great deal to find America in the biblical text.

Israel is the center of all biblical prophecy. It is also the land bridge between Europe, Asia, and Africa. Biblical history and prophecy are focused on Israel and its relationship to those nations that played a role in the Old Testament record.

Daniel's visions for the nations have to do with those nations' relationship to Israel. King Nebuchadnezzar took Daniel captive to ancient Babylon in 605 BC. While still a student in training, Daniel interpreted the king's dream about the great statue with a head of gold, arms of silver, belly of brass, legs of iron, and feet of iron and clay. According to the dream, the statue was obliterated by a great rock that filled the whole earth (Daniel 2:31-35).

As he stood before the great Nebuchadnezzar, Daniel told the king that God had revealed "what shall happen in days to come" (Daniel 2:28).* Daniel proceeded to explain that Nebuchadnezzar was the head of gold and that after him would arise three other kingdoms inferior to his own. Out of the fourth kingdom would come the ten toes, "partly strong and partly brittle" (verse 42). "In the time of those kings," Daniel explained, "the God of heaven will set up a kingdom that will never be destroyed...It will crush all those kingdoms and bring them to an end, but it will itself endure forever" (verse 44). Notice that the supernatural rock, cut out without hands, struck the ten toes of the statue.

About 50 years later, in 533 BC, Daniel had a vision in which he saw "four great beasts" come up from the sea (Daniel 7:3). These beasts represented the same four great empires Nebuchadnezzar saw in his dream. What Nebuchadnezzar saw as a beautiful statue, Daniel saw as wild animals about to tear each other apart. He saw a winged lion, which symbolized Babylon. Next came a lopsided bear, stronger on one side than the other. He later identified this second kingdom as Media and Persia (7:5; 8:20). The two arms of the statue and the lopsided appearance of the bear aptly described the dual empire that would eventually be dominated by Persia. Next, he saw a four-winged leopard, which he later identified as Greece (7:6; 8:21). Finally, he saw a fourth beast with ten horns (7:7). Its teeth were iron, the same metal as the fourth kingdom in the statue, and it subdued "whatever was left" by the others.

The Final Empire

Although Daniel never identifies the fourth beast, it is clearly Rome, the empire that succeeded Greece. The statue's two legs (2:33)

---

* All Scripture references in this section and under the next three subheadings are from the NIV.

seem to indicate the division of Rome into East (Greek-speaking Constantinople) and West (Latin-speaking Rome). The ten horns of this beast parallel the ten toes of the statue (2:39-43). They are identified as "ten kings who will come from this kingdom" (7:24), and after them "another king" will arise, an eleventh king, who will blaspheme God and persecute the saints. Many Bible scholars believe this person is the Antichrist.

Scholars generally agree that the ten horns of Daniel's fourth beast and the ten toes of the statue refer to the same thing. Both grow out of the fourth empire and represent the final phase of it. Premillennialists see a gap of time, the church age, separating the legs and toes, with the stone falling at the second coming of Christ at the end of Gentile history.

Daniel's prophecies clearly indicate the dominance of Israel by the Gentiles until the time of the Antichrist. Since Rome (the legs) and the revived Rome (the toes) of the last days are indicated by Daniel's prophecies, Daniel clearly points to Europe or the Roman Empire as the final Gentile power. Whether this final form of the fourth kingdom (the toes) includes America we can only speculate.

When Will This Happen?

The prophecy of the 70 weeks in Daniel 9 tells us that God put Israel's future on a timer. God told Daniel that 70 sevens (or 70 "weeks") are decreed for Israel and Jerusalem to finish its transgressions (verse 24). The prophecy continues by predicting that 7 "sevens" will pass as Jerusalem is rebuilt, and 62 more "sevens" will pass, for a total of 69, until the Anointed One (the Messiah) will be cut off. This leaves one "seven" left for the future.

Bible scholars generally interpret these "sevens" (Hebrew, *shavuah*) to refer to units of seven years. Seventy sevens would equal 490 years. Therefore, we can determine the span of time from Artaxerxes's decree for Nehemiah to rebuild Jerusalem (444 BC) to when the Messiah would be cut off (crucified) is 483 years (69 "sevens"). That would bring us to AD 32–33 on the Jewish calendar, depending on how the beginning and end years are calculated—the exact window during which Jesus was crucified, rose, and ascended back to heaven.

Daniel's Seventieth Week

This leaves one "week," or unit of seven years, yet to come. Many place this final seven years in the tribulation period, which will come after the rapture of the church. During these final seven years, God's prophetic clock for Israel will begin to tick again.

Notice that the prophecy of the 70 sevens was given to Daniel in regard to his people (the Jews) and their holy city (Jerusalem). All 490 years have to do with Israel rather than the church. This focuses our attention on the fact that Israel plays a prominent role in the tribulation period.

In the meantime, Daniel was told that "war will continue until the end" (9:26). That's what Jesus said in the Olivet Discourse (Matthew 24:6). We can conclude that the "times of the Gentiles" will be marked by wars and by the rise and fall of the four major empires presented in Daniel 2 and Daniel 7.

The Fall of Babylon

The prophecy of the fall of Babylon (Revelation 17–18) grabs our attention. It takes up two whole chapters in the Bible. In fact, the fall is actually announced earlier when an angel flies through the heavens and announces, "Babylon is fallen, is fallen" (Revelation 14:8). It is proclaimed twice for emphasis. The great kingdom of the end times, the kingdom of the Antichrist, will collapse and come under the judgment of God. This matter is so serious that an angel announces the judgment in chapter 14, and then the details are explained in chapters 17 and 18.

The Great Harlot

Revelation 17:1 teaches, "And there came one of the seven angels which had the seven vials, and talked with me, saying unto me, Come hither; I will show unto thee the judgment of the great whore that sitteth upon many waters." John is going to explain later that the "many waters" represent peoples. Revelation 17 presents a woman, the great harlot, who is the symbol of the leadership of the end times. She is a city that rules over the nations of the world. John describes her in symbolic language.

> So he carried me away in the spirit into the wilderness: and I saw a woman sit upon a scarlet colored beast, full of names of blasphemy, having seven heads and ten horns. And the woman was arrayed in purple and scarlet color, and decked with gold and precious stones and pearls, having a golden cup in her hand full of abominations and filthiness of her fornication (Revelation 17:3-4).

John the revelator is caught up into the distant future. He sees this woman, dressed in red and purple, on a scarlet beast, out in the wilderness. She is destined to rule the world. And she is empowered by Satan himself. Once again, we have the connection of the symbol of the seven heads and ten horns, which in the book of Revelation points to Satan himself, the power behind human governments and evil world systems. Then he begins to describe this individual in detail.

The symbolism in the book comes from the book of Daniel. Daniel was told that Babylon, Persia, Greece, and finally Rome would rule the world. Early Jewish and Christian scholars understood that prophecy to clearly point to the Roman domination of the world in ancient times.

Indeed, when we open the New Testament, we find Rome was ruling the world. Jesus was born in the days of Caesar Augustus, and the Jewish people were under Roman domination. A Roman governor, Pontius Pilate, sent Jesus to the cross. It was under Pilate, the Roman authority, that Jesus died for our sins on the cross. It was under the Romans that the early Christians often faced severe persecution. We have seen that the Old Testament predicted that would happen. But how does it relate to the New Testament? How does it relate to later Bible prophecies?

The Great Mystery

In Revelation 17:5, John gives us a description of this woman—the great city that rules the world in the end times. "And upon her forehead was a name written, MYSTERY, BABYLON THE GREAT, THE MOTHER OF HARLOTS AND ABOMINATIONS OF THE EARTH." Notice he makes it clear this is not literal Babylon. This Babylon presents a mystery. This is a mysterious, symbolic form of Babylon, a city that was, and is not, and yet shall ascend in the future according to verse 8. This city ruled the world, it ceased to rule the world, and it will rule the world yet again.

The final empire that was predicted in the Old Testament was the Roman Empire, the empire that sent Jesus to the cross. That was the empire that persecuted the early Christians and executed Paul and Peter. That empire began to disappear by the fifth century. And yet the influence of Roman systems in mathematics, in our language, and in our very alphabet still exists.

The Bible seems to be predicting the revival of the Roman Empire in the last days. "And here is the mind which hath wisdom. The seven heads are seven mountains, on which the woman sitteth" (Revelation 17:9). In the first century, anybody reading that would immediately identify the city on seven hills with Rome. In fact, first-century Christians were familiar with the *dea*—a coin that was minted by the Roman government and that made a goddess out of Rome itself.

Rome was pictured as a woman on those coins. If we read the Bible in the context in which it was originally written, we cannot miss the fact that John is identifying this city as Rome.

Some Bible readers argue that this image should be taken literally as a reference to Babylon in Iraq. They claim that one day, Babylon in Iraq will be rebuilt and rule the world. But think about that for a moment. Babylon sat 50 miles downriver from present-day Baghdad in an area that is now marked by instability and political upheaval. Would the European Union actually go to Iraq and set up its international headquarters under that kind of distress? That is highly unlikely. No, I think it is obvious that John is using Babylon as a symbol of Rome. He is using the woman, the beast, and the dragon as symbols of real things.

So Revelation 17 describes and predicts the fall of Babylon, the symbolic kingdom of the Antichrist, over which he will rule in the last days. Verse 9 tells us that he rules from the city that sits on seven hills. John's readers would have identified this with the city of Rome.

Verse 10 refers to seven kings—five have fallen, one is, and one is yet to come. This final one will continue for a short time. Some identify these as kings, and others view these as kingdoms. But the idea is that as Gentiles rule the world in the years to come, nations, kings, and empires will rise and fall. Eventually, a single ruler will emerge. The Old Testament calls him the "little horn" that pops out of the ancient kingdom of Rome (Daniel 7:8) and as the willful king (Daniel 11:36). The New Testament identifies him as the man of sin, the lawless one, the son of perdition, the beast, and the *antichristos*, the Antichrist himself. He is the one who will rule the world, and this is the kingdom through which he will rule.

Then notice what John says about the harlot and the dragon.

> These shall make war with the Lamb, and the Lamb shall overcome them: for he is Lord of lords, and King of kings: and they that are with him are called, and chosen, and faithful. And he saith unto me, The waters which thou sawest, where the whore sitteth, are peoples, and multitudes, and nations, and tongues (Revelation 17:14-15).

The Great City

So John is identifying for us the symbols in the passage. He wants us to understand who the great harlot is. He also wants us to understand what the great city is that rules over the kingdoms of the world. Then he goes on to explain that eventually, even the nations that are part of this kingdom, the ten horns that symbolize ten kings who all rule at the same time in the end times with the Antichrist, will turn against the woman, hate her, destroy her, and burn her with fire (Revelation 17:16). Who is this? "And the woman which thou sawest is that great city, which reigneth over the kings of the earth" (verse 18).

She is not necessarily a religious system. This is a material, economic, and social system that controls the world in the last days. The ancient Roman Empire controlled virtually all of modern Europe. It extended into parts of North Africa and the Middle East. But it was essentially a European empire. I think the Bible is making it very clear that this is the kingdom and the empire of the Antichrist, who rules over the world in the last days.

Notice the description and the destruction of this city: "And the kings of the earth, who have committed fornication and lived deliciously with her, shall bewail her, and lament for her, when they shall see the smoke of her burning" (Revelation 18:9).

Merchants will weep and mourn over her (verse 11). Sailors will stand afar off (verse 17). This city has political influence over the whole world. Kings and international leaders are sorrowing over the destruction of this city. Merchants are depending on it for their economy. They are sorrowing over its destruction. And even sailors are afraid to sail there in boats any longer. They sit offshore, watching the city burn.

One cannot sit in the Persian Gulf and watch Babylon in Iraq burn up. Modern Babylon is an archaeological excavation protected by military troops so people will not steal things from the site. It is not an active city ruling over the world today.

I have friends who maintain that this passage literally pertains to Babylon and teaches that one day Babylon will be rebuilt to be the greatest city in the world. But what does that say about the imminence of the rapture of the church? If the rapture could take place at any moment, Babylon would have to be rebuilt instantly. "Oh, a city can be built quickly," they reply. No, it can't—at least not in less than seven years, to the point where all the world is going to come to that city and trade with it. Following their logic, the merchants, sailors, military leaders, and political leaders of the world would all move their centers of operations to that one place in that short period of time. Is it possible? Anything is possible. Is it probable? No, it is not likely that this could happen so quickly.

I am willing to submit to God. God is God, and I am not. He can do anything He wants to do. But looking at our world realistically, it seems much more likely to me that this is a symbol of the great kingdom of the end times. I think biblical prophecy clearly connects it with Rome. The European Union may or may not include a relationship to America. But all of the economic development and prosperity of the world on which we depend so much for our own success, the Bible says, will one day all be destroyed. It will all be swept away. It will all be gone.

The Great Fall

We have examined what the Bible says about the great harlot, the great city. Now we want to take a look at the great fall that will come to that city in the last days. I realize these are serious prophecies. They tear our hearts. They rip our souls. But remember, this will happen to those who are left behind. This is not a warning for the church age. This is a warning for those who have been left behind in the time of the tribulation. But notice what Revelation 18:8 says about the great city that John symbolically refers to as Babylon: "Therefore shall her plagues come in one day, death, and mourning, and famine; and she shall be utterly burned with fire: for strong is the Lord God who judgeth her." In verse 9, the kings of the earth are mourning over her destruction. In verse 11, the merchants are mourning as well. In verse 17, the sailors are also mourning, for the smoke of her burning is going up as evidence of the judgment of

God. But notice what else that verse says: "For in one hour so great riches is come to nought."

That tells us that the judgment of the kingdom of the Antichrist will be total, permanent, and instantaneous. It will all be over in one hour, in one day. The Bible does not specifically say anything about nuclear war. But the only thing I can imagine that would destroy the greatest city in the world, the capital of the world's military, social, political, and economic prosperity, and wipe it out in one day, in one hour, would be a nuclear explosion. It is so bad, the merchants are afraid to go there. The sailors will not take their ships there. They will watch the smoke of the burning of the city go up in the air. They pull back in fear of what has happened. All of this, the Bible says, is the judgment of God on people. It does not occur simply because they loved their things. They did not love the God who made those things available to them.

As the merchants, the sailors, and the leaders all weep, notice what else the passage says: "Rejoice over her, thou heaven, and ye holy apostles and prophets; for God hath avenged you on her" (Revelation 18:20). Heaven rejoices while the world weeps. "And a mighty angel took up a stone like a great millstone, and cast it into the sea, saying, Thus with violence shall that great city Babylon be thrown down, and shall be found no more at all" (verse 21).

This is symbolic of the destruction of that city. This has never happened in history. It is yet to happen. That means that all the economic development of all these centuries of human history, all the material prosperity, all the great empires that have been built, all the great cities that have been built, all the great buildings that have been built, and all that man can possibly accomplish is gone in one hour in judgment and destruction. No wonder the apostle Peter said, "Seeing then that all these things shall be dissolved, what manner of persons ought ye to be in all holy conversation and godliness?" (2 Peter 3:11).

Only that which is eternal will last for eternity. And only a life that has been made coeternal with the life of God is going to spend eternity with Him. All of our efforts to build a great life, to build a great city, and to build a great society, no matter how well intended, ultimately will descend right back into the dust because without God, life has no meaning and purpose.

The whole point of the Bible is not to scare us about the future. It is to prepare us to be ready for the fact that Jesus is coming again to take His people home to heaven.

We are living in a day and age unlike anything the world has ever seen before. All of that change causes much concern and many questions, including the topic of our next chapter—the role of weapons of mass destruction in the end times.

12

WEAPONS OF
MASS DESTRUCTION

Bible prophecy looks down through the corridor of time and describes a terrible war that is yet to come. Men are fighting, armies are marching, the world is at war...and it sounds a lot like nuclear war. For example, Revelation 8:7 begins a description of the trumpet judgments. As the first angel sounded his trumpet of judgment, there fell on the earth "hail and fire mingled with blood," and a third of the trees and all of the grass were burned.

In verse 8, the second angel sounded his trumpet, and a great mountain or ball of fire fell into the sea, and a third of the ocean was polluted. In verse 10, a third angel sounded his trumpet, and the rivers were polluted—the fresh waters. In verse 12, the fourth angel sounded his trumpet, and a third of the sun, the moon, and the stars were darkened. The air was polluted.

As we read about these horrible ecological disasters of the end times, one thing becomes evident. If the air is polluted, the water is polluted, and the grass and the trees are burned, something of massive destruction is occurring on earth. These are not described in the Bible as natural ecological disasters. Nor are they described only as cosmic judgments, though that may be involved. They are the result of the world being at war at the time of the end. And the description of that war always has with it an emphasis of fire falling on mankind.

We have already seen what weapons of mass destruction can do. And it does not matter how many nations pledge to reduce the stockpile of weapons. Thousands of them remain on the planet today, many of them capable of mass destruction beyond anything the world has ever known.

The threat of nuclear war and international terrorism is the greatest challenge of our day and hour. Only a few years ago, the United States sought to stop Iran from "going nuclear." In 2013 Iran announced plans for 34 nuclear power sites. Several nations now have nuclear weapon capabilities—a scenario much different from previous generations, in which the United States and the Soviet Union were the only nuclear powers.

We are challenged by international terrorists, by the threat of nuclear weapons, and by the potential of mass destruction like never before in our history. Incident after incident keeps reminding us of the serious threat of the challenge we continually face.

Powerful Prediction

The Bible has a great deal to say about what is going to happen in the future. And one of its most amazing, stunning, and awesome prophecies contains predictions that sound like nuclear war. Today, India, Pakistan, and North Korea all have the potential to flood the world market with plutonium, highly enriched uranium, or actual nuclear bombs. It is only a matter of time until some tyrant will obtain a bomb and the means to deliver it and be willing to detonate it.

What happened in Hiroshima during World War II is only a microcosm of what will take place in the future. Today's nuclear weapons are far more powerful than their World War II–era ancestors. In addition, enough nuclear weapons now exist to destroy the entire planet several times over.

When we look at the Bible and its predictions about the future, one in particular refers to the possibility of the world being destroyed by fire. The apostle Peter says the flood destroyed the ancient world in the days of Noah. But then he tells us the world of the future will be destroyed by fire: "But the heavens and the earth, which are now, by the same word are kept in store, reserved unto fire against the day of judgment and perdition of ungodly men" (2 Peter 3:7).

In other words, Peter looks down through the corridor of time, into the distant future, and says, "A time is coming when the world will be destroyed by fire. It is reserved for that final judgment." Then he begins to explain the event in detail. He reminds us that God is "not willing that any should perish, but that all should come to repentance" (verse 9). That is the desire of the heart of God. But for those who do not come to repentance, who do not come to surrender their lives to the Lord, judgment will come. Verse 10 says, "But the day of the Lord will come as a thief in the night." The phrase *the day of the Lord* refers to the Battle of Armageddon, the time of the end, the final future judgment.

The rest of verse 10 reads, "The heavens shall pass away with a great noise, and the elements shall melt with fervent heat, the earth also and the works that are therein shall be burned up." The Bible does not specifically mention nuclear war by name, but this certainly sounds like it. Examine closely the elements of verse 10. There will be an explosion in the heavens. In verse 12, the elements of the earth will "melt with fervent heat." The earth itself will be destroyed. Those ominous predictions certainly sound as if they refer to nuclear war.

The judgment of God could come in cosmic fashion. It could come as a result of human war. It could come as a direct divine judgment from God Himself. But as Peter describes this, he seems to be saying, "The world is at war, and that war is the judgment of God." God will withdraw His hand of protection and allow all hell to break loose on the earth as a judgment against the ungodliness of men.

> Seeing then that all these things shall be dissolved, what manner of persons ought ye to be in all holy conversation and godliness, looking for and hasting unto the coming of the day of God, wherein the heavens being on

fire shall be dissolved, and the elements shall melt with
fervent heat? (2 Peter 3:11-12).

In the light of all of this, Peter goes on to say that we look forward to a new heaven and a new earth. He is not saying, "Let's just
hurry up and blow up the world." Christians have never wanted that.
We want peace. We want the nations of the world to come to resolution with one another. We would hope for a window of grace, for
God to extend time for people to come to repentance and to faith.
That is the intent of the passage.

Remember who Peter was—he was Jesus's disciple. This is the
fisherman himself, who followed the Lord. On one occasion he
denied the Lord, and then he was reinstated. He became the leader
of the early church. He preached the famous sermon on the Day of
Pentecost in which 3000 people were saved. Keeping these things
in mind, we realize Peter understood the heart of God. God does
not want to see the destruction of the earth. God is calling people
to repent, to come to peace and to resolution with God Himself.
But the Bible says that if they do not, then in the time of the end, as
people turn away from God, they invite the judgment of God. And
the judgment of God will cause the world to be destroyed one day.

In Revelation 8, we have what are called the trumpet judgments.
The seven angels of God sound their trumpets, one immediately
after another. And the judgment of God falls on the earth during
the tribulation.

> And the seven angels which had the seven trumpets pre-
> pared themselves to sound. The first angel sounded, and
> there followed hail and fire mingled with blood, and
> they were cast upon the earth: and the third part of trees
> was burnt up, and all green grass was burnt up (Revela-
> tion 8:6-7).

This ecological disaster sounds like nuclear war.

"And the second angel sounded, and as it were a great mountain burning with fire was cast into the sea: and the third part of the sea became blood" (verse 8). A third of the oceans were polluted.

Then the third angel sounded his trumpet in verse 10. A star fell from the heavens to the earth, and a third of the rivers were polluted. In verse 12, the fourth angel sounded his trumpet, and a third part of the sun, the moon, and the stars were smitten, and darkness prevailed on the earth for a third of the time.

Proliferation of Weapons

In each of these four trumpet judgments, one-third of the entire planet is affected. This is no ordinary war from ancient times. Nothing like this has happened in all of history. This is a prediction of what will happen in the future. It is a time of incredible judgment that is coming on the planet in the future, a time when the proliferation of weapons is out of control.

The book of Revelation makes it clear that all of the battles, wars, and conflicts it describes will eventually lead to the Battle of Armageddon (Revelation 16:16). Old Testament prophets said basically the same thing. In Joel 3:2,11-12 we read that the nations will surround the city of Jerusalem. In Zechariah 14:2-3,12-15 we learn of a future war with Israel in the center. In Zephaniah 3:6-8, we have a prediction of a final conflict that involves the nations of the world against Israel in the last days.

All of these battles and conflicts tell us that the world is headed toward a final, unprecedented time of conflict. These predictions are so severe and serious, they will result in a whole series of battles that the Bible describes as the time of tribulation, the time of distress, the time of trouble. The Battle of Armageddon will spread from the Valley of Jezreel north of Jerusalem, into the city of Jerusalem itself, to the Valley of Jehoshaphat, and all the way south toward Edom.

We have in the Scriptures serious prophecies about what is going to happen in the future. These are described as divine judgments, but as we read the details in the book of Revelation, we see armies marching and men fighting. The world is at war.

Mankind has engaged in thousands of wars. The world has often been at war. There were two major world wars in the twentieth century alone. In the twenty-first century we are dealing with the war against terrorism as we face the threat of international terrorism and possibly the use of nuclear weapons by terrorists. All of those things seriously challenge our sense of freedom, peace, and stability for the future. So we have to ask ourselves, where is the world today in light of what the Bible predicts about the future?

The Scripture makes it clear that we are not to set any dates for the end of the world or the coming of Christ. Certainly, the Bible itself does not give such a date or such a prediction, but it does tell us the end will come one day. As humanity spins out of control, the anger and hostility of various nations will come to the forefront, led by religious insanity that thinks it is serving the purposes of God by creating war. We are going to face this challenge more seriously than ever in the days ahead.

In the meantime, we need to pray for peace, work for peace, hope for peace, and pray for our leaders, that somehow peace might prevail in our time. But we also realize that the human ability to restrain the depravity of the human heart is limited. As more and more people turn away from God, they invite His judgment on our world.

People view tragic events of our time and ask, if God exists, how could He allow this to happen? First, yes, God does exist. Second, if anything should surprise us, it is the fact that He has not judged us more severely already. You cannot continue to live out of control, violate the commandments of God and the principles of the Scripture, turn your back on God, act as though He does not exist, cast off all restraint in your behavior, and then expect God to bless you. That is not going to happen.

No, the further people get away from God, the more they invite His judgment. The judgment of God will finally come when He simply withdraws His hand of restraint. Suddenly, the depravity of the human heart will be completely uncontrolled, and people will be on the verge of destroying one another.

I know we do not like to think about this. But it is the reality of our times. What is the ultimate problem that fuels the threat of nuclear disaster? The Bible itself shows us the root of the real issue and the real problem.

The Problem of Depravity

Human depravity is what ultimately fuels war, anger, devastation, and destruction. Mankind has the intelligence to create a nuclear bomb—it's merely a matter of scientific exploration. However, what we do with that weapon is a matter of the human heart. And the Scripture makes it very clear that the real problem society is facing in the world today is the problem of the depravity of the human heart. Jesus Himself commented on this in the Sermon on the Mount.

> Ye have heard that it was said by them of old time, Thou shalt not kill; and whosoever shall kill shall be in danger of the judgment: But I say unto you, That whosoever is angry with his brother without a cause shall be in danger of the judgment (Matthew 5:21-22).

In other words, anger in the human heart leads to murder, destruction, and devastation. The Old Testament book of Proverbs tells us that "an angry man stirreth up strife" (29:22). He is out of control. The result of his anger can lead not only to personal conflict in the family but also to international conflict in war.

Jesus's own brother said, "Where envying and strife is, there is confusion and every evil work" (James 3:16). When people are

unable to control their anger, it leads to conflict, and conflict leads
to war. That happens on an international scale. It can also happen on
a personal level. Notice how the apostle Paul explains the progres-
sion of evil. He enjoins us to eliminate these things from our hearts.
"Let all bitterness, and wrath, and anger, and clamor [yelling at each
other], and evil speaking [blasphemy] be put away from you, with
all malice" (Ephesians 4:31).

Malice is the deliberate attempt to harm somebody else. When
people get angry, upset, and out of control, when they are yelling
and screaming and blaspheming one another, it is only a matter
of time before all that uncontrolled anger leads to malice. It leads
people to say, "I'm going to deal with you. I'm going to hit you. I'm
going to hurt you. I'm going to kill you." That eventually leads to
war.

The problem in the hearts of many people around our globe
is not that they are not intelligent enough to deal with the challenges of the political processes. It is not that they are not intelligent enough to lead their military with a sense of control. No, it is a
problem of anger. It is that deep-seated anger in the heart. We see it
manifested all over the world. Unfortunately, we see it all too often
in the Middle East. Out-of-control religious anger says, "I'm going
to kill you in the name of God." The individual making such a threat
believes he is doing God a favor, but the God of the Bible teaches
us exactly the opposite.

What the world really needs is a change of heart. America needs
a spiritual revival, making our hearts right with God and therefore
right with one another. When we watch the news about the threat
of terrorism or weapons of mass destruction, we are concerned—
and rightly so because it is a reality. But some of us cannot even get
along with one another. Some of us cannot even get along with family members. There is war in the home. War in the home needs to
be resolved in the heart, just as the resolution of any war or conflict
must be a spiritual matter of the heart.

The God of the Bible went out of His way to tell us He loves us. God did not create us to be destroyed, or to destroy ourselves, or to destroy the world. God said He created us in His likeness and His image so that we might have a relationship with Him, so that we might be in fellowship with Him, and so that we might know His love, grace, power, and peace in our own souls. When your heart is at peace with God, you can learn to get along with everybody else and be at peace with others.

That is not always easy. Sometimes that requires a willingness to forgive someone who has hurt you and wronged you, a willingness to forgive somebody who really does not want to communicate with you. But you will find that when you put the principles of the Word of God to the test, they always work. When you learn to love your enemy as yourself, when you learn to forgive, and when you learn to cooperate, you will find yourself suddenly stepping out of your comfort zone and into a zone where God is at work in your life and the power of God can be demonstrated in your own personal experience.

For some of us, it's time to stop being mad at God and to make peace with Him. For some of us, it's time to stop being mad with one another and to make peace with each other. For our leaders, it's time to learn to make genuine peace in the world in which we live.

Sometimes, peace must come through strength. But strength should be used with control and restraint to the glory of God. Strength exists not just to express the anger in our hearts and the frustration in our lives, but to fulfill God's purpose in our lives. God has a great purpose for the world in which you and I live. Jesus tells us clearly that He went to the cross to die for the sins of the world. His death on the cross makes possible the reconciliation of all people to one another. Regardless of who you are or where you are, God's ultimate purpose for your life is to bring you into a peaceful relationship with Himself so that you might be at peace with yourself and with the world.

Reflecting on the Five Prophetic Signs

Step back for a moment and reflect. If you wanted to understand how soon something were going to take place, wouldn't you look at preliminary events that set the stage for that event to occur? For example, let us say you decide to go to a concert. You arrive at the venue, but nothing is happening. The lights are off, and nobody seems to be doing anything. Nobody is setting up the orchestra. Nothing is happening on the stage. You would probably think you had the wrong date.

But suddenly somebody turns on the lights. People appear and start setting up the chairs and music stands. The players begin to show up and warm up their instruments. You decide you had the right date after all because you see the stage being set for the event.

Or suppose you go to a baseball game. The lights are out in the stadium. Nothing is happening. The teams are not out there warming up. You wonder if there really is going to be a game today. But then the lights come on, the teams show up, and they begin to warm up. The stage is being set, and the game will soon begin.

That is what we have in Bible prophecy. These five signs tell us the stage is already set. We do not know the exact timing. Jesus made that very clear. "Of that day and hour knoweth no man, no, not the angels of heaven, but my Father only" (Matthew 24:36). Somebody will always come along and say, "Well, it doesn't say the year, so let's guess the year." No, it means nobody knows the time. Don't waste your time trying to guess the time. Be ready all the time because Jesus could come at any time!

The rapture could occur at any moment. We see the signs of the return already on the horizon, so we expect the rapture to happen sooner rather than later. Remember, if the signs of Christmas are already at the mall, that tells us that Thanksgiving is coming even sooner.

Review these five signs: Israel is back in the land. The Middle East is in crisis. The global economy is already a reality. The European

Union already exists. And the weapons of mass destruction have already been invented. How much more do I need to know to wake up and realize we are closer to the end than we have ever been? It is as though God is shouting to us from both the Bible and the newspaper, telling us to get ready because the end is coming.

PART 3

THREE PROPHECIES
THAT PROVE THE BIBLE IS TRUE

The Bible is under attack today like never before. People question its historicity and authenticity. They question its authority and spirituality. But we will consider three prophecies that prove the Bible is indeed true and that it is what it claims to be—the Word of God that speaks with power and authority to our lives.

Scripture itself claims, "All scripture is given by inspiration of God, and is profitable for doctrine, for reproof, for correction, for instruction in righteousness: that the man of God may be perfect, thoroughly furnished unto all good works" (2 Timothy 3:16-17).

"Produce your cause, saith the LORD…declare us things for to come" (Isaiah 41:21-22). Then He added, "I am God, and there is none else; I am God, and there is none like me, declaring the end from the beginning, and from ancient times the things that are not yet done…I have spoken it, I will also bring it to pass; I have purposed it, I will also do it" (Isaiah 46:9-11).

God assures us that we can know that He alone is God because He alone can predict the future.

Does the Bible really prove to be true when we look at its prophecies? The answer is yes, absolutely. In our final three chapters, we'll look at three prophecies that prove the Bible is accurate on matters regarding both the past and the future.

13

THE GROWTH OF THE CHURCH

The first undeniable prophecy that proves the Bible is true is Jesus's prediction of the continual growth of the church. We live 2000 years after He made this prediction. History has witnessed the growth of the church. But when Jesus gave this prophecy, the church did not exist. When He took those disciples aside in Matthew 16, He left the borders of Israel and traveled to the town of Caesarea Philippi, a very Gentile and pagan place. Caesarea Philippi was named for Caesar and for Herod Philip. The city was known for idolatry. The Greeks believed that a steam that came out of a huge rock marked the gates of hell itself.

Jesus went to this place, stood in front of that massive rock where the steam came out in ancient times, and proclaimed to Peter in the hearing of the disciples, "Thou art Peter, and upon this rock I will build my church; and the gates of hell shall not prevail against it" (Matthew 16:18).

Jesus realized that His current ministry strategy—sending the disciples to announce to the nation of Israel that He is the promised Messiah—would come to an end. His own people would reject Him, and He would turn to the Gentiles. He would later say to the disciples in the Great Commission, "Go ye therefore, and teach all nations" (Matthew 28:19).

Jesus's great prediction in Matthew 16 foreshadows those developments.

People tend to read this verse as though hell were attacking the church and the church had to somehow hold out to the end. But a gate is not an offensive weapon—it is used for defense. Jesus pictures Satan on the defensive, hoping the gates to his hellish kingdom can withstand the onslaught of the church. Jesus means for the church to be on the attack—not with guns and instruments of war, but with the power of the message of the good news of the gospel. We declare, God loves you, Christ died for you, He rose from the dead, and He is coming again.

This is a message of personal transformation. "I will build my church" could more literally be translated, "I will build My church and keep on building it and keep on building it"— until God calls the church home to heaven.

The Rapid Growth of the Early Church

The story of the birth of the church is recorded in Acts 2. On the Day of Pentecost, when the Spirit of God came on those early Christians, they began to declare the Word of God with boldness. On that day, 3000 people were saved and baptized in the name of Jesus the Savior.

The account of the birth of the church in Jerusalem provides a beautiful report of the initial fulfillment of Christ's prediction.

> And they continued steadfastly in the apostles' doctrine and fellowship, in the breaking of bread, and in prayers. Then fear came upon every soul, and many wonders and signs were done through the apostles. Now all who believed were together, and had all things in common, and sold their possessions and goods, and divided them among all, as anyone had need.
>
> So continuing daily with one accord in the temple, and breaking bread from house to house, they ate their food with gladness and simplicity of heart, praising God and having favor with all the people. And the Lord added to the church daily those who were being saved (Acts 2:42-47 NKJV).

The church grew from 120 to 3120 in one day! After that, the Lord caused this first church to grow each day. Acts 4:4 tells us that about 5000 men had become Christians. Including families, the entire church could have included more than 20,000 people. All of this took place within about two years and without buildings and modern technology.

In addition, the early church experienced much persecution. When Stephen became the first martyr, the entire church fled Jerusalem except the apostles (Acts 8:1). But as Pastor John MacArthur notes, the church continued to grow.

> That tremendous growth continued, although being a Christian back then wasn't easy. The price was high, the demands were extreme, and total commitment was essential. But after having counted the cost, many were still coming to Christ. There's nothing wrong with tremendous growth if it's the result of evangelism—that's the only kind of growth that is real. Those Christians wanted to win others to Jesus Christ, and empowered by the Holy Spirit, they did. Their only motive was God's glory, so the Holy Spirit magnified their work. Later in Acts when Paul and Barnabas reported the conversion of Gentiles, "they caused great joy unto all the brethren" (15:3). There's nothing more exciting to the people of God than being used by God to draw others to Himself.[1]

God used even this struggle to grow His church. During this time, the gospel began to spread beyond the Jews to Gentile (non-Jewish) people wherever these Christians fled. For example, when the Samaritans heard Philip's preaching, "the people with one accord gave heed" (Acts 8:6).

Acts 9:31 reports, "Then had the churches rest throughout all Judaea and Galilee and Samaria, and were edified; and walking in the fear of the Lord, and in the comfort of the Holy Ghost, were multiplied." By the time Paul wrote the book of Romans only about

25 years after the resurrection, a small but vibrant church already existed in the capital of the empire.

New Testament scholar N.T. Wright provided a colorful explanation of this growth.

> The origin of Christianity is actually itself one of the most extraordinary phenomenon in the history of the world. In AD 20 there's no such thing as a Christian church. By AD 120, the emperor in Rome is getting letters of worry from one of his proconsuls in northern Turkey about what to do about these Christians. So in that century, you have this extraordinary thing suddenly appearing out of nowhere. All the early Christians for whom we have actual evidence would say, "I'll tell you why it's happened. It's because of Jesus of Nazareth and the fact that He was raised from the dead."[2]

Kenneth Latourette notes the rapid growth of the church despite persecution in the first five centuries following the resurrection.

> Due to a lack of information, it is impossible to calculate accurately the growth of the Christian church during the first centuries. However, we know that within five centuries Christianity became the dominant religion of the Roman Empire. The Jesus-movement, which started in an obscure part of the Roman Empire, in a relatively short period transformed into a major religion with millions of followers spread out from India in the east, Ethiopia in the south to Britain in the west.[3]

A Time of Transition

A transition took place from the old dispensation and old covenant (to the Jews) to the new dispensation and new covenant (to Jews and Gentiles alike). Jesus's great prediction, "I will build my church," provided a bridge to the fulfillment of the Great Commission, "Go ye therefore, and teach all nations, baptizing them in the name of the Father, and of the Son, and of the Holy Ghost" (Matthew 28:19). The plan of God is to call out a church unto Himself.

The Greek word translated *church* is *ekklesia*, from which we get the Spanish word *iglesia*. It means to call (*kaleo*) out from (*ek*, as in *exit*)—to call out people for yourself and assemble them together. So the translation can be "the assembly," "the congregation," or in the Scottish language, "the *kirk*," which then becomes in English, "the church." It means that God is calling a people for Himself out of the world of unbelievers. He has promised to assemble us and empower us so that the gates of hell will not prevail against us. After 2000 years, two billion people have claimed that Jesus Christ is their Savior, that He is the One they are following, and they have put their hope for heaven and eternity in Him.

Remember, when Jesus made the prediction, there was no church. There was only a handful of believers among the disciples. Yet Jesus dared to say that He would build His church, that it would prevail even against the gates of hell, and that the church would continue to grow until the trumpet sounds, the archangel shouts, and the Lord calls us home to glory.

So the ministry of the church began at Pentecost and will end at the rapture. In between, we should not be surprised that the disciples took the gospel to Asia Minor, Greece, Rome, Europe, and eventually the entire world—North America, South America, Africa, Asia…The message of Christ has spread all over the world and continues to spread today. It has been attacked and persecuted, and believers have been martyred. But the church continues to grow in fulfillment of Jesus's prophecy, proving the Bible indeed is true.

What Should We Be Doing?

We can never be certain when God's purposes for His church will be finalized, so we must remain obedient to our Lord's commands regarding His church. This was made clear to the disciples when Christ ascended to heaven. They had asked if He was going to restore the kingdom to Israel at that time, and Jesus told them, "It is not for you to know the times or dates the Father has set by his own authority" (Acts 1:7 NIV). Two facts are clear in this statement: The date has been set, and we aren't supposed to know it because we have a responsibility to fulfill in the meantime.

In the very next verse, Jesus reiterated the Great Commission, telling the disciples they would be empowered by the Holy Spirit to be His witnesses in Jerusalem, Judea, Samaria, and "to the ends of the earth" (Acts 1:8 NIV). Then, to their amazement, He ascended into heaven, leaving them gazing intently into the sky. Two men in white (probably angels) appeared and asked, "Why do you stand here looking into the sky? This same Jesus, who has been taken from you into heaven, will come back in the same way you have seen him go into heaven" (verse 11 NIV).

All too often, today's Christians are just like those early disciples. We spend more time gazing into the sky and speculating about Christ's return than we do serving Him. The angels' point was to remind the disciples that His return is certain. Thus we shouldn't waste time and energy worrying about when or whether Christ will return. Believe that He is coming again—on schedule—and be about His business in the meantime.

Jesus left several instructions about what we ought to be doing while we await His coming:

- *Witness for Him everywhere you go.* Our Lord told His disciples to be His witnesses everywhere—even to the farthest ends of the earth (Acts 1:8).

- *Go into all the world and preach the good news* (Mark 16:15). This command emphasizes the evangelistic and missionary ministry of the church in the present era. We are to take the gospel to the whole world.

- *"Repentance for the forgiveness of sins will be preached in his name to all nations"* (Luke 24:47 NIV). Calling men and women to repent and believe the gospel is the twofold nature of the evangelistic enterprise.

- *"Make disciples of all nations, baptizing them,"* Jesus said in Matthew 28:19 (NIV). Making converts and discipling them in their walk with God is a major emphasis of the church's mission.

- *Build the church in every generation.* Jesus told His disciples that He would build His church with such power that "the gates of hell shall not prevail against it" (Matthew 16:18). Jesus intended the church to be on the march until He calls her home.

- *"Work...until I come back"* (Luke 19:13 NIV). In the parable of the talents, Jesus said the servants were to put their master's resources to work until he returned. We are to stay busy about the Master's business until He returns.

- *Remain faithful until He returns.* Near the end of His prophetic message in the Olivet Discourse, our Lord reminded His disciples to continue in faithful and wise service even though He might be gone a long time (Matthew 24:45; 25:14-21).

Is There Any Hope for Our Generation?

Genuine spiritual revival is the result of the outpouring of the Holy Spirit on the church. Throughout history, God often has moved to bless His people in a fresh and powerful way. Genuine revival came as God's people were convicted of their sin, repented, and gained a new zeal and devotion for God in their lives. In revival, the self-centered, halfhearted indifference that so often dominates our lives is swept aside by a new and genuine desire to live for God.

Revival renews our values and redirects our lives. It calls us to a more serious walk with Christ and results in substantial and abiding fruit (see John 15:16; Galatians 5:22-23). The changes that occur in individual believers and in the church speak convincingly to the world about what it really means to belong to Christ. Such revival comes when God's people pray, when God's truth is proclaimed, and when God's Spirit moves in our lives.

Unfortunately, we see little evidence of genuine revival today. Some have lost hope of it altogether. Others have diluted the gospel message in order to make its appeal more acceptable to today's generation. Bailey Smith has made this observation:

> The Christ of the Bible has been reduced to a fallible humanitarian. Salvation has been repackaged into a feel-good experience. Forgotten in today's "gospel revisionism" is the message that sent Christ to the cross and the disciples to martyrdom. Today's gospel "lite" is hardly worth living for and certainly not worth dying for.[4]

If we are going to make an impact on our generation for the cause of Christ, we must do it now. We have no idea how much time is left, so we dare not let the time slip away indiscriminately. If we are going to use wisely whatever time God gives us, we must be about His business with a sense of urgency. On one hand, we dare not presume on God's grace by assuming we have plenty of time left to get the job done. On the other hand, we dare not ignore the grace of God by assuming it is too late for our generation.

Prophecy lovers are especially prone to this second reaction. We are eschatological pessimists. We know all too well that things eventually are going to get worse, not better. We believe that a growing religious apostasy is strangling the spiritual life of our churches. And we have little hope in human efforts to revitalize our dying culture. This can sometimes lead to a kind of eschatological fatalism. If we are not careful, we can abandon our calling and just sit and wait for the rapture. But there is no biblical warrant for such fatalism. The Bible never tells us that things will be so bad that we should give up, quit preaching altogether, and wait for the end. Rather, the Bible clearly instructs us to keep preaching, testifying, and witnessing, knowing that Christ will continue to build His church until He comes.

In the meantime, we can live with our eyes on the skies, watching for Christ to come, and with our feet on the earth, working for Him until He comes. This balance of expectation (that Jesus could come at any moment) and participation (serving Him faithfully until He comes) is what the Christian life is really all about. Living in the light of His coming keeps us focused on what is really important in life. It also keeps our attention on the balance between our present responsibilities and our future expectations.

The hope of the second coming is the strongest encouragement for us to live in righteousness until Jesus comes. The ultimate incentive to right living is the fact that we will face our Lord when He returns. Each of us needs to be ready when that day comes. If we faithfully live out whatever time is left to us, we will surely hear Him say, "Well done, good and faithful servant!"

Two Streams of Bible Prophecy

There are two streams of prophecy in the Bible that are absolutely opposite each other. On the one hand, Jesus said, "I will build my church; and the gates of hell shall not prevail against it." The apostles risked their lives by taking the message of the gospel to all the world, preaching that Jesus is the Savior, and calling people to put their faith and trust in Him. In fact, the apostle Paul said he was praying that there would be glory in the church by Christ Jesus throughout all ages, world without end (Ephesians 3:21). And indeed, there has been. From Pentecost to the rapture, Jesus's great prediction is being fulfilled as the church continues to grow today.

It should not surprise us, then, that we now have the largest churches in history. For example, the *Outreach* magazine 2013 list of the largest churches in America includes 11 churches with a weekly attendance of more than 20,000 people. Dr. Warren Bird's list of the world's largest churches includes many congregations around the globe with 50,000 or more members.[5] Several house church networks among the underground church in China represent tens of thousands of believers. The gospel is making a difference for the cause of Christ around the world. The church continues to grow.

As we'll see in the next chapter, this stream of prophecy has a darker counterpart, and both streams testify that the Bible is utterly trustworthy.

14

THE SPREAD OF EVIL

In addition to the growth of the church, Jesus also predicted that there will come a time when the spread of evil will be worse than it has ever been in all of history. He said, "Many false prophets shall rise, and shall deceive many. And because iniquity shall abound, the love of many shall wax cold" (Matthew 24:11-12).

In other words, as sin becomes worse and worse, the love of many will grow cold. The hearts of people will grow cold toward God, the things of God, and the Word of God. We are living in a day and age of unbelief, skepticism, and of atheism such as the world has never seen. People are belligerently saying, "There is no God, there is no heaven, there is no hell, there is no final judgment, there is no accountability. We are nothing more than animals, the product of the evolutionary process. The only thing that matters in life is me, myself, and I—whether I'm happy and whether I can get what I want out of life."

Seemingly each day we hear of a religious leader who was involved in a financial scandal or who committed some form of immorality. Many Christian denominations and organizations are changing their standards to permit various forms of evil unthinkable in previous generations. They seem to have thrown the Bible out the window. Yet this falling away in the church is an important end-time development—the rise of the apostate church. It includes a departure from the truth, a deceptive message, and a distortion of the gospel. None of this should take us by surprise, for the Bible predicted all of it.

Departure from Truth

Scripture warns us to beware in the last days of the rise of apostasy, when people step away from long-held biblical traditions, doctrines, and truths, turn their backs on the things of God, walk away from God, and promote themselves in the place of God.

One of the most powerful and stunning prophecies of the end times is that of the rise of the apostate church. Consider this prediction by the apostle Paul, warning young Timothy of what to expect in the future.

> Now the Spirit speaketh expressly, that in the latter times some shall depart from the faith, giving heed to seducing spirits, and doctrines of devils; speaking lies in hypocrisy; having their conscience seared with a hot iron (1 Timothy 4:1-2).

It is as though they do not even care that the commandments of God and the principles of God are taught in the Bible. They throw all that out the window. Their attitude is, "We're going to do what we want to do anyhow. I want to live the way I want to live. I don't care what the Bible says about decency, morality, right and wrong, standards for the ministry, or anything else."

Instead, people are promoting themselves. Even now, people do not even have the decency to conduct a church service with respect and dignity. Every marketing tactic of the business world has been adopted to "make church relevant." One *Christian Post* headline even offered this shocking headline: "Pastor Says 'Church Sucks,' Mixes Worship with Katy Perry, Maroon 5; Tells Congregation Not to 'Get Its Panties in a Bunch.'"[1]

Ultimately, however, the question is not the style of the worship—it's the content of the message. The true message of Scripture reminds us that we are all sinners who need to come to repentance, salvation, and faith in the blood of the Lord Jesus Christ. It is the blood of Christ that saves and changes a life. We are not saved by self-effort, self-promotion, positive thinking, or simply trying to live a better life. People can try those all they want, but they will never work. The real change in the heart and soul of an individual comes only from God Himself.

Scripture contains other warnings of apostasy as well. Paul also wrote to Timothy about the character of people in the days ahead.

> This know also, that in the last days perilous times shall come. For men shall be lovers of their own selves, covetous, boasters, proud, blasphemers, disobedient to parents, unthankful, unholy, without natural affection, trucebreakers, false accusers, incontinent, fierce, despisers of those that are good (2 Timothy 3:1-3).

They hate the cause of truth and righteousness. If a preacher today stands up for what is right and emphasizes biblical morality, he will be criticized, attacked, and mocked. He will be rejected by society as a bigot, a small-minded individual who "just doesn't get it" and lacks understanding of how life really is.

But Scripture makes it clear that "how life really is" is destroying our world and will ultimately destroy the planet. Paul goes on to say people will be "lovers of pleasures more than lovers of God; having a form of godliness, but denying the power thereof" (verses 4-5). They are still religious. They have not rejected church altogether. They have not totally walked away from God. But they are trying to bring God down to the level of a human being. They are trying to remake God into the image of man instead of realizing that men are created in the image and likeness of God. God's purpose and intention is to save the soul, transform the heart, and change the life so that we might live godly lives and make a difference in the world in which we live.

But all too often, in many of our churches, there is no difference between the person in the pew and the person on the street. There is no difference between the person who professes to be religious and the person who says, "I don't have time for God at all." We need revival if we are going to see a difference come to America in these last days. America needs repentance. America needs transformation. It is time to stop indulging ourselves and to get on our knees, turn to the God of heaven, and call on Him to make a difference in our lives while there is still hope this side of the rapture.

We have every reason to believe that the gospel will be preached, souls will be saved, lives will be changed, and the church of Jesus Christ will go on successfully until the time of the end. But as we get closer to that time, attitudes of self-indulgence, self-centeredness, self-promotion, and greed will increase. People will treat God as if He were a puppet on a string, as if they could pull the string and make Him do whatever they want.

We need to understand that God is God, and we are not. God will do what He is going to do. We cannot force God to do anything. We can submit to God, surrender to God, pray to God, call on God, and trust God to meet our needs. But the knowledge of God consists of a relationship between a fallible human being and the infallible Creator of the universe. When I entrust myself to His hands and put my life and my future under His care, I can have hope for the future. But if church is really all about me—"Come to our church. It's fun!"—people will miss the main goal of worship. All of those things may be well and good in their place. But if that is all there is, it is no different from any other group or club. On the other hand, the message of Jesus Christ is, "If any man will come after me, let him deny himself, and take up his cross, and follow me" (Matthew 16:24).

Deceptive Message

The future apostasy of the church is clearly predicted as a precursor to Christ's second coming. The apostle Paul tells the young church at Thessalonica not to be tricked into thinking Christ had already returned, for "the day of Christ…shall not come, except there come a falling away first" (2 Thessalonians 2:3).

The term *falling away* translates the Greek term *apostasia*, from which we get the word *apostasy*. It means to stand away from something or depart from it, such as departing from a standard of truth. It would be like someone saying, "I believe this to be true" and then turning around and walking away from it. He would depart from it. He would stand away from it. He would deny what he once affirmed.

You can argue all day long whether the people who fall away had their salvation and lost it or whether they were never saved in the first place. Either way, the end result is still the same. Somebody professing to be a believer suddenly begins to preach and proclaim that which is not the message of the gospel.

Paul also writes, "For I am not ashamed of the gospel of Christ: for it is the power of God unto salvation" (Romans 1:16). His dependence on the truth of the gospel stands in stark contrast with the attitude of the apostate church. "That man of sin [will] be revealed, the son of perdition; who opposeth and exalteth himself above all that is called God, or that is worshipped; so that he as God sitteth in the temple of God, showing himself that he is God" (2 Thessalonians 2:3-4).

The apostasy of the church paves the way for the coming of the Antichrist, the sinister world ruler of the future. As the church gets away from the simple message of the gospel of the Lord Jesus Christ, unbelief will enter in and capture the hearts and minds of people. Scripture tells us that when people deny the essential message of the gospel, professing to become wise, they become fools (Romans 1:22). God will give them up to uncleanness. If they do not repent, God will give them up to vile affections, and then ultimately to a reprobate mind (Romans 1:24-28).

The deceptive message of the future will be a message of self-acceptance, self-absorption, and self-promotion. It will forget the

God of the Bible. The Bible is not just a book about how to make life better for me. It's about my coming into an experience with the God of heaven, who changes and transforms me. We do not just need more positive thinking. We need genuine repentance—people getting on their knees and their faces before God and recognizing, "I have sinned. I have failed. I need Your help. I need Your forgiveness. God, only You can save my soul. Only You can change my heart and life. Only You can give me the proper direction to know how to live life effectively for the future."

When the Scripture tells us an *apostasia*—an apostasy, a falling away, a departing from the truth—is coming, beware and be prepared. The apostasy will pave the way for the Antichrist. How will that work? Second Thessalonians 2:7 refers to "the mystery of iniquity," or the mystery of lawlessness, which is already at work—but somebody is restraining it, holding back the arrival of the wicked one. That someone is the Holy Spirit Himself. The Spirit of God restrains evil in the world through the preaching of the message of Jesus Christ so that the gospel might go forth and so that the church might be built to the glory of God.

But eventually, the Scripture says, the Restrainer will be removed. That is certainly a reference to the rapture of the church, when the trumpet sounds, the archangel shouts, the dead in Christ are raised, and we who are alive and remain are caught up into the presence of God. That will occur in the future. When it does, all hell will break loose on the earth. The apostasy will take full effect. The Antichrist, the wicked one, will come to power. His nature and power will then be revealed. But ultimately, the Lord will consume him with the brightness of His coming and the power of His spoken word (2 Thessalonians 2:8).

Paul says the coming of the man of sin is "after the working of Satan" (verse 9). We should not be surprised, then, that some churches today that have claimed for centuries that they believed the message of the Bible and believed in the person of Jesus Christ now suggest that maybe Jesus is not really divine after all. Maybe He did not really say the things Scripture claims He said. Maybe the four Gospels don't really contain the words of Christ Himself. Perhaps the message of a moral transformation is no longer needed in society. We are getting further and further away from the essential message of Scripture. And the Bible says in the end, the deceptive message will result in strong delusion: "God shall send them strong delusion, that they should believe a lie" (2 Thessalonians 2:11).

We are on the verge of seeing that happen in our society more severely than ever in history. People are no longer convinced that they are sinners in need of the message of salvation. They are no longer convinced that there is a heaven to gain and a hell to avoid. Rather, they want to know how their lives can be better, how they can find some peace, joy, and happiness. Let me remind you, they will never find it apart from the Prince of Peace, the One who is the expression of the love, grace, and joy of God Himself.

Distortion of the Gospel

Apostasy means walking away from the truth, standing away from that which you once believed. Apostasy occurs when the message of the gospel is distorted. We have a biblical example of the apostle Paul dealing with the possibility of apostasy among some of his converts.

Paul preached the gospel of the grace of God, the message of salvation through faith, in the province of Galatia. Yet later he had to write a letter to the Galatians as if to say, "What in the world happened to you? You've messed it up. You've made a mistake."

"I marvel that ye are so soon removed from him that called you into the grace of Christ unto another gospel" (Galatians 1:6). The Greek word translated *I marvel* is *thaumazo*. It is filled with power and passion. "I'm shocked," Paul said. "I can't believe it. You believed the message of salvation by grace, and now you're walking away from that to another gospel?" He also uses the Greek word *heteros* ("different"), from which we get the term *heretic.* It's not a similar gospel. It's a totally different gospel. It is a distortion of the message of the gospel of the grace of God. But he immediately says "It is not another" (verse 7). Here he uses the Greek the word *allos,* which means "another of the same kind."

Paul is saying, "The gospel you are preaching now is not another gospel of the same kind. 'You know, we're just changing it a little bit to make it fit our day and age.' No, it's not the same. It's a different gospel—a completely different, heretical, unorthodox gospel. It is *heteros,* not *allos.* It perverts the gospel of Christ."

Then in very strong words, he says, "But though we, or an angel from heaven, preach any other gospel unto you than that which we have preached unto you, let him be accursed" (verse 8). The word *accursed* is the Greek word *anathema.* Paul is saying, "Let him be under the judgment of God."

Paul took the gospel very seriously. He was confronted by the risen Christ on the road to Damascus. He threw himself to the ground and cried out, "Lord, what do You want me to do?" Jesus spoke to him personally and called him to be His disciple. Paul understood, "My salvation is not based on my good works. I can't work my way to heaven." That is another gospel. Paul was a sinner who had persecuted Christians. He had even condemned them to death. He was opposed to the things of Jesus Christ. But he came to faith in Christ and received the gift of salvation by faith, just as any other sinner must receive it.

When people pervert the gospel, several things happen. Some people want to add to the gospel. They claim that in addition to believing that Jesus died for your sins, you have to do some additional things and follow certain practices and principles in order to get to heaven. The other extreme is to subtract from the gospel. "Oh, you don't even need to worry about what you believe. Jesus loves you no matter what. You'll make it to heaven."

The Scripture warns us in a number of places that people will be deceived in the last days. The Bible describes these people in several ways.

- *Liars.* They will even lie to themselves.
- *Heretics.* They will preach a *heteros* (completely different) gospel.
- *Scoffers.* They will scoff at the things of God, especially the idea of Christ's second coming.
- *Blasphemers.* They will blaspheme the God of the Bible, the commandments of the Bible, and the principles of Scripture.
- *Seducers and reprobates.*

That's a heavy list. The Bible is emphatic when warning us that false prophets and false teachers will arise in the last days. Eventually a false church, an apostate church, will carry on religious functions but will not honor the message of Christ. The message will be utterly different from the true message that Jesus Christ is the Son of God, who stepped into the human race in human flesh. He is God incarnate, God on foot, God among us. He went to the cross, suffered, bled, and died on our behalf. He took on Himself the sins of the world. He died, not as a martyr, not as a victim of circumstances, but as the Lamb of God, who carried the sins of all mankind. He rose from the dead in a literal resurrection, walked out of the tomb, showed the scars of the wounds on His hands and feet to the disciples, and said to them, "Be not faithless, but believing. Thomas, put your finger in the nail print, and see that it is really Me."

Scripture says that same risen Christ who ascended into heaven shall so come again in like manner as the disciples saw Him go (Acts 1:11). He will return one day to reign and rule on this earth. That is the message of the Bible.

I don't know what church you go to. If it is preaching the message of Jesus Christ, if people are coming to salvation in Christ and into a personal relationship with Him, if your church is standing for biblical truth and biblical morality, then you need to give your time, your heart, your service, and your money, supporting your church and supporting the cause of Christ on earth.

But perhaps you are going to a church that no longer preaches and teaches those things. It has turned into a social club. It is mixed up and confused about the simple message of salvation through the blood of Jesus Christ and the grace of God. That is apostasy. Or maybe your church tells you that you have to be baptized only in that church and nobody else's, that you have to join that membership and nobody else's, that everybody else is wrong but that church, then beware. That is not the gospel either.

Invest your life, your time, and your attention in a church that is being established to the glory of God. One day, as the apostasy gets worse and worse, the trumpet will sound. The archangel will shout. And the Lord Jesus will call the true church home to heaven. The real question is, when He comes, is He coming for you?

Everything that is going wrong in the world today ought to tell us that the Bible is true. The prediction is being fulfilled. Yes, according to one stream of prophecy, the church is continuing to proclaim its message and grow. But at the same time, according to another prophetic stream, evil is getting worse and worse. Good and evil are on a collision course with each other. That is why American society is so divided today. That is why some people are concerned about righteousness and about the things of God, but other people are not only unconcerned, they even hate the idea of righteousness, hate the Bible, and hate the things of God.

As we change the channels on television from one reality show to another, we can listen to people curse, yell, and scream at one another, making selfish choices and decisions to benefit only themselves. That alone ought to tell us something is wrong with the soul of our nation. We are in serious trouble. But it also points out that the Bible is true. Exactly what the Bible said was going to happen is happening. We are not evolving into a greater consciousness of global awareness, brotherly love, and concern. We are degenerating toward self-destruction.

15

THE RETURN OF CHRIST

Is there any hope then for the future? Yes, there is! A third undeniable prophecy will be fulfilled that will finally convince the
world beyond any shadow of a doubt that the Bible is true. The
final prophecy that will settle it once and for all is the prediction of
the return of Christ. When Jesus ascended into heaven, two angels
appeared to the disciples and said, "This same Jesus, which is taken
up from you into heaven, shall so come again in like manner as
ye have seen him go into heaven" (Acts 1:11). Jesus ascended into
heaven literally, bodily, and physically. He ascended into glory. And
the Bible says He will return one day literally, bodily, and physically
in power and great glory.

Jesus Himself predicted this would occur "after the tribulation
of those days"—those days in the future, those days of vengeance,
those days of judgment after the rapture of the church, those days
when the wrath of God will be poured out on an unbelieving world.

> Immediately after the tribulation of those days shall the
> sun be darkened, and the moon shall not give her light,
> and the stars shall fall from heaven, and the powers of
> the heavens shall be shaken: and then shall appear the
> sign of the Son of man in heaven: and then shall all the
> tribes of the earth mourn, and they shall see the Son of
> man coming in the clouds of heaven with power and
> great glory (Matthew 24:29-30).

The final evidence of the truthfulness of biblical prophecy is the return of Christ Himself. That will finally prove that the Bible is true. However, it will prove this to a generation for whom it is too late. For those who have been left behind, wrath and judgment will fall. The book of Revelation makes that clear over and over again. Christ, the Lamb of God, will open the seals of judgment on an unbelieving world—the wrath of the Lamb. God will pour out the bowls of judgment at the time of the end—the wrath of God. The unbelievers on the planet will run, hide, cry, scream, and curse, but they will not pray. The Bible repeats, "And they did not repent," "and they did not believe" in spite of all that. This will be a time of terrible tragedy. But the final apologetic proof of the truth of Scripture will be the return of Christ, when He comes back in power to judge the earth.

The Bible tells not only of Christ's return but also of the glories of those who trust in Him. The final two chapters of the Bible speak clearly of what will take place following the rapture, the tribulation, the return of Christ, and His millennial reign. Satan will be defeated and sin will be removed. God describes in beautiful detail what lies ahead for those who believe. We will live in a new heaven and new earth, dwelling together in perfect community with God and His people in the Holy City, the new Jerusalem.

The Holy City

The final prophecy in the Bible describes the coming of the new Jerusalem, the Holy City. As the book of the Revelation comes to a close, we come down to the very end of time and the beginning of eternity future. All the judgments have finally come to completion. All the nations have come to stand before the Lord Himself. The saved have entered into heaven. The lost have been cast into the lake of fire. In the final two chapters in the Bible, John the revelator looks down the corridor of time into the distant future and sees the new heaven, the new earth, and the new Jerusalem. "And I saw a new heaven and a new earth: for the first heaven and the first earth were passed away; and there was no more sea" (Revelation 21:1).

There will be no more oceans. People debate whether the new heaven be a reconstitution of the old heaven and earth or something brand new. If there is no ocean, there is no plankton. The environment does not sustain life the same way it does on the earth today. This implies that it is a whole new place.

Then John says, "And I John saw the holy city, new Jerusalem, coming down from God out of heaven, prepared as a bride adorned for her husband" (verse 2). This is a picture of the ultimate dwelling place of the bride of Christ, the heavenly city, which will be all that God ever intended the earthly Jerusalem to be. It will be far better, far greater than anything that we could ever imagine.

"And I heard a great voice out of heaven saying, Behold, the tabernacle of God is with men, and he will dwell with them, and they shall be his people, and God himself shall be with them, and be their God" (verse 3). The promise in this passage of Scripture is for every saved person who has ever lived. Old Testament saints, church-age saints, tribulation saints, millennial saints…all the people of God for all the ages of time are there in the family of God in the eternal city. Here the bride of Christ is the great new city of Jerusalem itself.

> And God shall wipe away all tears from their eyes; and there shall be no more death, neither sorrow, nor crying, neither shall there be any more pain: for the former things are passed away. And he that sat upon the throne said, Behold, I make all things new. And he said unto me, Write: for these words are true and faithful (verses 4-5).

This is the new eternity, the new heaven, the new earth, the new Jerusalem, the ultimate experience of the people of God. John uses two entire chapters to describe this place to us so that we can begin to comprehend what it is like. The water of life is there. The tree of life is there. The blessing of God is there. But more than anything else, God is there. Verse 11 reveals that the glory of God lights the city. It is resplendent with the glory of God Himself.

Come hither, I will show thee the bride, the Lamb's wife.
And he carried me away in the spirit to a great and high
mountain, and showed me that great city, the holy Jerusalem, descending out of heaven from God, having the
glory of God: and her light was like unto a stone most
precious, even like a jasper stone, clear as crystal (verses
9-11).

That is the light of the city. In fact, John will go on to say that
the city will not need the sun or the moon for light, for the glory of
God and the Lamb will be its light (verse 23). Think of what that
means. In the Old Testament, the glory of God, the Shekinah glory,
resided on the Ark of the Covenant. Only the high priest could
enter the Holy of Holies and stand in the presence of the glory of
God. When Moses saw the reflected glory of God, God said to him,
"I cannot look at you face-to-face. You will not be able to live if you
stand in My presence." And the reflected glory of God glowed on
the face of Moses.

God will be in the eternal city, the new Jerusalem. "And they
shall see his face" (Revelation 22:4). What a promise! There in the
presence of God, you will become a priest of God, a king with
Christ, to reign and rule with Him through all eternity. The promise
of Scripture is that Jesus rules in our hearts now in the church age. In
the millennial kingdom, Jesus will rule on earth for 1000 years. But
then, in eternity, we will rule with Him forever and ever, adminis-
tering His lordship over a universe that is beyond our imagination.

The nearest stars are 4.3 light-years away. You couldn't get there
in several lifetimes. And yet in eternity, you will have countless ages
to explore the vast universe. In the new Jerusalem, you will be dis-
covering new worlds, new places, and new things that are presently
beyond your imagination, forever and ever.

The description of the Holy City of new Jerusalem is one of the
most amazing descriptions in one of the greatest prophecies in the
Bible. Look again in Revelation 21. Notice that verse 12 says the city

had a great, high wall and 12 gates. At the gates were 12 angels, and on the gates were the names of the 12 tribes of the children of Israel.

Note verse 14. The city wall has 12 foundations, which are named for the 12 apostles of the Lord Jesus. In other words, the heavenly city will encompass the entire family of God. It is for saved Jews and Gentiles. It is for those who knew the Lord in the Old Testament dispensation and those who know the Lord in the New Testament dispensation. The gates of the city are named for the 12 tribes of Israel. The foundations are named for the 12 apostles. All of this reminds us that the entire family of God will be there for all eternity.

Then John says in verse 16 that the city lies "foursquare." It is as wide as it is long as it is high. It is like a gigantic cube 1500 miles wide and high and deep. It would quite easily accommodate the billions of people who have come to know Christ as their personal Savior over the centuries. All of the family of God is there.

Then John tries again to describe the indescribable. He uses the analogy of precious stones, listing and naming each one (verses 19-20). Many of these were found on the breastplate of the high priest of Israel. Those stones symbolize this great future city. Then John says in verse 22, "And I saw no temple therein."

Here is an overview of the description of this city.

> It's bright as jasper, clear as crystal (21:11),
>> and made of pure gold, like clear glass (verses 18,21).
> It's surrounded by a wall 220 feet high (verse 17).
> Its gates are
>> named for the 12 tribes of Israel (verse 12),
>> made of giant pearls (verse 21),
>> and always open (verse 25).
> It's 1,500 miles high, wide, and deep (verse 16).
> God and the Lamb live there (verse 22)
>> and give it light (verse 23),
>> so it has no night (verse 25).

The saved of all nations live there (verse 24),
and nothing that defiles will enter (verse 27).

The Heavenly Temple

If this is the Holy City, where is the heavenly temple? The heavenly temple is the pattern in heaven of the earthly temple down below. But the heavenly temple here is described in a totally different way. "And I saw no temple therein: for the Lord God Almighty and the Lamb are the temple of it" (Revelation 21:22).

God Himself is the temple. We will dwell there with Him and in Him in His presence. In the earthly temple, the high priest could not enter the Holy of Holies except on the Day of Atonement. The other priests couldn't go farther than the Holy Place, and laymen were limited to the courtyard. In heaven, no one is limited. Everybody has access into the presence of God Himself. That is the holy temple of the new Jerusalem.

"And the city had no need of the sun, neither of the moon, to shine in it: for the glory of God did lighten it, and the Lamb is the light thereof" (verse 23). In these closing chapters of the book of Revelation, we see the Lamb, Christ, sharing the throne, the temple, and the holy city with God the Father. We see that the Son is coequal with the Father. The emphasis is on the deity of Christ throughout these passages. And verse 24 tells us who is going to be there: "And the nations of them which are saved shall walk in the light of it: and the kings of the earth do bring their glory and honor into it."

Only the saved will enter into the new Jerusalem. Only the saved will be in the new heaven and the new earth. Only the saved will participate in the family of God for all eternity. Then John gives us a list of who is not going to be there—that which defiles and works abomination and makes a lie (verse 27). In other words, those who have never been saved, whose hearts have never been transformed, and whose eternal destiny has never been changed will not be there.

The good news is, anyone who wants to come into the presence of God in heaven may come. The final invitation of Scripture is to whoever will come (Revelation 22:17). But the bad news is that those who do not choose to come, those who do not put their faith and trust in Christ, will be excluded. They will not be there. All of the lost and unsaved will not be there.

The saved of the nations will be there in heaven for all eternity. The promise is to every believer—all whose names are written in the Lamb's book of life (21:27). Having your name written down in heaven, in the book of life, secures your eternal destiny in heaven.

John continues his description in chapter 22. "He showed me a pure river of water of life, clear as crystal, proceeding out of the throne of God and of the Lamb" (verse 1). And then in verse 2, "There was the tree of life." That has not appeared in the Bible since Genesis 3, when Adam and Eve were banished from Eden. The tree of life is the symbol that paradise is regained in the heavenly city, in the Holy of Holies, in the heavenly temple. There, the people of God have access to the presence of God, to the life of God, and to the power of God.

The Highest Heaven

The Bible describes the new Jerusalem as the highest heaven. The apostle Paul said in 2 Corinthians 12 that he was "caught up to the third heaven." He was not referring to the atmosphere around the planet, the clouds, or outer space, but to the dwelling place of God. That is the place being described for us here in the book of the Revelation.

John may be describing the city literally when he mentions the stones, jasper, gold, and gates of pearl. Or he may be using human language to describe the indescribable, something beyond our anticipation or recognition. But the most important thing is stated in Revelation 22:3—"There shall be no more curse." The curse of sin is gone. The curse of death is removed.

In addition, "The throne of God and of the Lamb shall be in it; and his servants shall serve him: and they shall see his face" (verses 3-4). The phrase "see his face" was a first-century idiom that referred to an audience with the king. The average person never saw the king face-to-face. If you had an audience with the king, you could look right into his face. John is telling us that in heaven, we will have an ongoing audience with the King. God's own face will finally be revealed to believers for all eternity.

Then John tells us our purpose in the new Jerusalem. We will be God's servants forever. We will not just float around endlessly in heaven. We will be busy serving the Lord (verse 3) and reigning with Him forever (verse 5 says). The eternal reign of the believer is pictured here in the new Jerusalem. We will be busy serving God. We will reign and rule with Him over the incomprehensibly vast expanse of the universe. God is currently giving us just a glimpse of what is out there. Ultimately, we will see it all. We will not need a rocket to get from one part of the universe to another. No, we will have time and opportunity to do it all, to see it all, and to experience it all.

In this life, people often want to travel and see the world. People have their bucket list of things to do before they die. Let me assure you, we will have millions and millions of things to do for all eternity, when we will not die. That is the promise of the Bible. Eternal life is the gift of God. Those who live forever will serve Him forever. They will reign with Him forever. They will be there forever. What a promise!

John begins to wrap up the entire book of the Revelation with this: "I am Alpha and Omega, the beginning and the end, the first and the last. Blessed are they that do his commandments, that they may have right to the tree of life, and may enter in through the gates into the city" (Revelation 22:13-14). Next John records this instruction and invitation: "I Jesus have sent mine angel to testify unto you these things in the churches. I am the root and the offspring of

David, and the bright and morning star" (verse 16). Jesus is instruct-
ing us to preach this in the churches. He commands that prophecy
serve as an important part of the church's teachings.

John then closes with these words from God: "And the Spirit
and the bride say, Come. And let him that heareth say, Come. And
let him that is athirst come. And whosoever will, let him take the
water of life freely" (verse 17). I hope you have accepted this invitation from the Lord. I hope your mind has been stirred, your heart
has been blessed, and your soul has been challenged. These biblical truths will bless your life. God will use them not only to inform
your mind but also to change and transform your walk with Him
and empower you to share them with others. Let me encourage you
to continue reading the final section of this book as a response to
these 15 future events that will shake the world and that can change
your future—starting today.

A FINAL WORD:
HOW TOMORROW
IMPACTS TODAY

The timing of the last days is in God's hands.[1] From a human viewpoint, we appear to be standing on the threshold of the final frontier. The pieces of the puzzle are all in place. As the sands of time slip through the hourglass of eternity, we are all moving closer to an appointment with destiny. The only question is, how much time is left?

The tension between living for today and looking for tomorrow is one of the realities of the Christian life. We often find ourselves caught between the here and now and the hereafter. On one hand, we need to be ready for Jesus to come at any moment. On the other hand, we have God-given responsibilities to fulfill in this world in the meantime.

We are living in a time of great crisis, but it is also a time of great opportunity. We must be prepared for the challenges that lie ahead of us. New technologies will make our lives more convenient, but we will also become more dependent on them. Medical advancements will continue to pose enormous ethical challenges. The shifting sands of sociopolitical change will also challenge our national and international policies in the days ahead. We will soon find ourselves living in a very different world from the one into which we were born. All of these changes and challenges will confront us in the days ahead.

Five Unshakable Pillars

Each one of us must prepare for Christ's return. No one else can get your heart ready to meet God. You and I must do that ourselves. Jesus urges us to do three things in view of His second coming:

> Keep watching (Matthew 24:42).
> Be ready (Matthew 24:44).
> Keep serving (Matthew 24:46).

Erwin Lutzer, the senior pastor of Moody Church in Chicago, identifies "five unshakable pillars" to enable us to live with eternity in view.[2]

God still reigns.

Human leaders will come and go. Some will be better, some worse. Some will be what we deserve—a reflection of our own weakness and sinfulness. But behind the scene of human governments, God still reigns over the eternal destiny of mankind. Beyond this temporal world, God rules from the throne in heaven. He guides His children and overrules in the affairs of men and nations to accomplish His will and purposes. The Bible assures us that "there is no authority except that which God has established" (Romans 13:1).* Regardless of who our leaders are, we are to offer "prayers, intercession and thanksgiving…for kings and all those in authority" (1 Timothy 2:1-2).

The church is still precious.

During this present age, God is still working through His church to evangelize the world. Jesus gave us clear direction about what we are to be doing until He returns: "Go and make disciples of all nations, baptizing them in the name of the Father and of the Son and of the Holy Spirit, and teaching them to obey everything I have commanded you…to the very end of the age" (Matthew 28:19-20).

---

* Except where noted, Scriptures quoted in this chapter are taken from the NIV.

The church may flourish or be persecuted in the days ahead, but she is to be faithful to her mission until Jesus calls her home to glory (1 Thessalonians 4:13-17).

Our mission is still clear.

The church stands as the salt and light of God in society. We are to "declare the praises of him who called you out of darkness into his wonderful light" (1 Peter 2:9). Lutzer suggests that we can accomplish this by...

- representing Christ to the world through a godly lifestyle
- winning people to Christ through intellectual and moral confrontation with loving persuasiveness
- strengthening our families as a testimony to God's grace

The integrity of sincere and authentic Christian lives and families speaks volumes to a lost world that is desperate for meaning and purpose. We cannot underestimate the spiritual impact that true Christianity has on those who have no answers to the overwhelming problems of life. When Christians live out their faith with authenticity and boldness, they capture the attention of the watching world.[3]

Our focus is still heaven.

Modern American Christians can easily forget that heaven is our real destiny. So many believers today live in such peace and affluence that they forget about heaven. We actually think that God's purpose is to bless our lives here on earth. Dave Hunt observed, "Unfortunately, too many persons—even dedicated Christians—find heaven a topic of only minor interest because they consider it irrelevant to the challenges of this present life."[4] We must remember, however, that this world is no friend to grace. As time passes, we should expect a continual moral decline in secular society. The Bible reminds us that there will be an "increase of wickedness" and that "terrible times" will come in the last days (Matthew 24:12; 2 Timothy 3:1). In the meantime, whatever success we have in this world must be measured in the light of our eternal destiny. Joseph Stowell reminds us that making heaven our primary point of reference will transform our relationship to everything that is temporary in this world.[5] C.S. Lewis wrote, "Christians who did most for the present world were just those who thought most of the next."[6]

Our victory is still certain.

The ultimate Bible prophecies focus on the triumph of Christ and His bride, the church (Revelation 19). They assure us that we will share in His victorious reign. Whatever transpires in the meantime must be viewed in light of our eternal destiny. Peter Marshall, former chaplain of the US Senate, said, "It is better to fail at a cause that will ultimately succeed than to succeed in a cause that will ultimately fail."[7] Until the trumpet sounds and the Lord calls us home, we have the Great Commission to fulfill and the world to evangelize. There is no reason to let up now. We have no clear date for the termination of the present age, so we must keep on serving Christ until He comes.

A young African martyr wrote these words in his prison cell before he died:

> I'm part of the fellowship of the unashamed, the die has been cast, I have stepped over the line, the decision has been made—I'm a disciple of Jesus Christ—I won't look back, let up, slow down, back away or be still.
>
> My past is redeemed, my present makes sense, my future is secure—I'm finished and done with low living, sight walking, smooth knees, colorless dreams, tamed visions, worldly talking, cheap giving and dwarfed goals.
>
> My face is set, my gait is fast, my goal is heaven, my road

is narrow, my way is rough, my companions are few, my guide is reliable, my mission is clear. I won't give up, shut up, let up until I have stayed up, stored up, prayed up for the cause of Jesus Christ.

I must go till He comes, give till I drop, preach till everyone knows, work till He stops me and when He comes for His own, He will have no trouble recognizing me because my banner will have been clear.[8]

A Date with Destiny

The world is speeding toward its ultimate date with destiny. Every day that passes moves us closer to the end. The people and the planet have a divine appointment to keep. As the clock of time ticks away, mankind comes closer and closer to earth's final hour.

It is only a matter of time until our planet will be plunged into the most devastating catastrophe imaginable. The outcome is certain. Global conflagration is clearly predicted in biblical prophecy. The only real question is, how much time is left?

Almost 2000 years ago, the apostle Peter said, "The end of all things is near. Therefore be alert and of sober mind so that you may pray" (1 Peter 4:7). Way back in the New Testament era, Peter and the other apostles sensed that they had moved dramatically closer to the consummation of God's plan for this world. The Old Testament age had come to an end, and they were now part of a new era.

Peter's reference to the end is expressed by a perfect-tense verb in the original Greek text. This means the action involved is a present reality with future consequences. It could just as appropriately be translated, "The end of all things has already begun." For Peter, the end of the age was already a present reality.

The first coming of Christ initiated the end of the age (see Acts 2:14-20; Hebrews 1:2), and His second coming will terminate the end of the age (Matthew 24:30). Therefore, the entire church age is a "last days," or a "last of the last days."

Scripture also speaks of the end as a future event. The apostle Paul predicted, "There will be terrible times in the last days" (2 Timothy 3:1). The opening verse of the apocalypse refers to "things which must shortly come to pass" (Revelation 1:1 KJV) and goes on to warn us that "the time is near" (Revelation 1:3). Scripture also presents Christ's coming as an imminent reality. "Look, I am coming soon!" Christ promised (Revelation 22:7). He will come suddenly, and He could come at any moment.

That leaves us asking, what time is it now? Peter referred to the present, saying, "[Christ] was revealed in these last times" (1 Peter 1:20). But Peter also referred to the coming of Christ as a future event, "ready to be revealed in the last time" (1 Peter 1:5). It is clear that he viewed the last times as both a present reality and a future event.

The Bible affirms three basic facts about the coming of Christ at the end of the age.

We are living in the last days. Every generation of Christians has lived with the hope of the imminent return of Christ. We believe that He could return at any moment. There is no prophetic event that remains to be fulfilled before the way can be opened for Him to return. In fact, certain events, including the return of Israel to her land, indicate that we are close to the end.

God's timetable is not our timetable. Peter told us that "in the last days scoffers will come" and question the promise of Christ's second coming (2 Peter 3:3-4). They will reject the idea of God's intervention in human history and suggest that all things are moving forward at their own pace without God. These skeptics will also fail to anticipate God's coming judgment on the world (verses 8-9). God's perspective is not limited to human time. But we dare not mistake the patience of God for a change in His plans. He is waiting, giving His people time to repent. The Bible warns, "He who is coming will come and will not delay" (Hebrews 10:37).

Christ's coming is always growing closer. The Bible emphatically promises that Christ is coming again (Luke 12:40; Philippians 3:20; Titus 2:13; Hebrews 9:28). Scripture urges us to be watching, waiting, and ready for our Lord to return. Every day that passes brings us one day closer. Whether He returns next week or 100 years from now, we are to be living as though He were coming today.

Looking Ahead

Anticipation is the key to preparation. If you were expecting an important visitor, you would probably keep looking for him to arrive. You would probably make preparations for his visit. Your anticipation of the visitor's arrival would influence your preparation for his visit. The same is true of our anticipation of the coming of Christ. If we really believe He is coming, we will want to be prepared for Him when He comes.

Jesus illustrated this in His own prophetic teaching with the story of the ten virgins (Matthew 25:1-13). Only those who were prepared for the wedding were invited into the banquet. The others were left out. Jesus used this illustration to remind us to keep watch because we don't know the time of His coming. Dr. John Walvoord comments on this passage, "The important point here... is that preparation should precede the second coming of Christ and that it will be too late when He comes."[9]

If we can take seriously the biblical predictions about the end time, then we must make preparation now for what is coming in the future. We cannot wait until all other options have been exhausted. The time for action is now. If you are not sure about your own relationship with Christ, make sure before it is too late.

Many things demand our attention in life. Many voices are calling to us, and many images flash across our minds. But regardless of our focus in life, one thing is certain—all of us will face death sometime. We cannot avoid it. All of us are vulnerable.

Death is the great equalizer. It makes no difference how rich or poor, famous or infamous, respected or rejected you may have been in this life. When you face death, you are facing an impartial judge. The Bible reminds us that "all have sinned" (Romans 3:23) and "the wages of sin is death" (Romans 6:23). When death comes knocking at your door, all that really matters is that you are ready to face it.

The reason Jesus came the first time was to die for our sins. He came to pay the price for our sins so that we might be forgiven. He is called our Redeemer because He has redeemed us from God's judgment against our sin. The apostle Peter wrote, "You were redeemed… with the precious blood of Christ…He was chosen before the creation of the world, but was revealed in these last times for your sake" (1 Peter 1:18-20).

Put Your Faith and Trust in Christ Today

The Bible tells us we can know that we have eternal life. With absolute certainty, we can know that Jesus died on the cross, that He rose from the dead, and that He is coming again. We can know whether we have said yes to Him. Going to heaven is not a matter of guesswork or chance: "I hope I'm going to make it…I think I've done the right thing…" No, Jesus did the right thing when He went to the cross and died in your place, when He took the wrath of God against you on Himself, and when He rose from the dead to give you the gift of eternal life. You and I must put our faith and trust in what He did. The Bible is telling us the truth that "everyone who calls on the name of the Lord will be saved" (Romans 10:13).

You can know that you are ready to meet the Lord because you have chosen to put your faith and trust in Him. If you want to make that decision today, I urge you to call on Him right now. You might want to pray something like this sincerely from your own heart.

> *O God, I know I need a Savior. I know I need Your forgiveness. And I really do believe that Jesus died in my place, that He rose again, and that He is coming again. I want to know for sure that He is coming for me. And today, I am committing my heart, life, and soul to Him.*

If you are making that decision for the very first time today, please let me know. I would like to send you some material that will help you as you begin your new walk with Christ.

Ed Hindson
The King Is Coming
PO Box 907
Colton CA 92324-0901
www.thekingiscoming.com

NOTES

Chapter 1: Millions Missing

1. Millard Erickson, *Christian Theology* (Grand Rapids: Baker Books, 1985), p. 1186.

Chapter 3: World Peace Promised

1. Grant Jeffrey, *Prince of Darkness* (Toronto: Frontier Research, 1994), pp. 48-55.
2. Cited in Jeffrey, *Prince of Darkness*, p. 53.
3. Richard Trench, *Synonyms of the New Testament* (New York: Cosimo Classics, 2007), p. 107.
4. See Charles Feinberg, *Daniel* (Chappaqua, NY: Christian Herald Books, 1981); Robert Culver, *Daniel and the Latter Days* (Chicago: Moody Press, 1954); Stephen Miller, *Daniel: New American Commentary*, vol. 18 (Nashville: Broadman & Holman, 1994); John Walvoord, *Daniel: Key to Prophetic Revelation* (Chicago: Moody Press, 1971); John Whitcomb, *Daniel* (Chicago: Moody Press, 1985).
5. Miller, *Daniel*, p. 307.
6. Feinberg, *Daniel*, pp. 174-75.
7. Arno Froese, *How Democracy Will Elect the Antichrist* (Columbia, SC: Olive Press, 1997), pp. 113, 138-39.
8. Harvey Cox, *The Seduction of the Spirit* (New York: Simon & Schuster, 1973), p. 16. See also Ed Dobson and Ed Hindson, *The Seduction of Power* (Old Tappan, NJ: Revell, 1988).
9. Arthur W. Pink, *The Antichrist* (Minneapolis: Klock & Klock, 1979), p. 77.
10. Jeffrey, *Prince of Darkness*, pp. 29-30; see also Pink, *The Antichrist*, pp. 83-88.
11. J. Dwight Pentecost, *Things to Come* (Grand Rapids: Zondervan, 1965), p. 339.
12. See Mal Couch, ed., *Dictionary of Premillennial Theology* (Grand Rapids: Kregel, 1996), p. 117.
13. Thomas Ice and Timothy Demy, *Fast Facts on Bible Prophecy* (Eugene: Harvest House, 1997), p. 77.
14. Ice and Demy, *Fast Facts on Bible Prophecy*, pp. 78-79.
15. Samuel Andrews, *Christianity and Anti-Christianity* (Chicago: Moody Bible Institute, 1898), p. 320.

Chapter 4: Two Dead Men and a Nation Come to Life

1. J. Hampton Keathley III, "The Temple, the Two Witnesses, and the Seventh Trumpet," Biblical Studies Foundation, 2004, bible.org/seriespage/temple-two-witnesses-and-seventh-trumpet-rev-111-19.

Chapter 5: The Dome of the Rock Destroyed

1. Tim LaHaye, *Revelation Unveiled* (Grand Rapids: Zondervan, 1999), p 184.

2. More information on this topic is available in my article "Rebuilding the Jewish Temple," www
.bibleprophecyblog.com/2013/10/rebuilding-jewish-temple.html#ixzz2huslMkpC.

3. "Blueprints revealed for the Third Jewish Temple," Israel Unseen, May 12, 2013, www.israelu
seen.com/blueprints-revealed-for-the-third-jewish-temple/.

4. Grant Jeffrey, *The New Temple and the Second Coming* (Colorado Springs: Waterbrook Press,
2007), chapter 5.

5. John Ankerberg and Jimmy DeYoung, *Israel Under Fire* (Eugene: Harvest House, 2008),
pp. 104-6.

6. Jeffrey, *The New Temple and the Second Coming*.

7. "The Nascent Sanhedrin," TheSanhedrin.org, www.thesanhedrin.org/en/index.php/The
_Nascent_Sanhedrin.

8. "The Re-established Jewish Sanhedrin," TheSanhedrin.org, www.thesanhedrin.org/en/index
.php?title=The_Re-established_Jewish_Sanhedrin.

9. Arnold Fruchtenbaum, *Ariel Ministries Newsletter*, Fall 2004/Winter 2005, p 4.

Chapter 9: The Middle East Crisis

1. This chapter is adapted from Ed Hindson and Tim LaHaye, "The Israeli Factor," chap. 7 in
Global Warning (Eugene: Harvest House, 2007).

2. On the biblical history of Israel, see Alec Motyer, *The Story of the Old Testament* (Grand Rapids:
Baker, 2001); Walter Kaiser, *A History of Israel* (Nashville: Broadman & Holman, 1998); Eugene
Merrill, *Kingdom of Priests* (Grand Rapids: Baker, 1987); K.A. Kitchen, *On the Reliability of the
Old Testament* (Grand Rapids: Eerdmans, 2003).

3. On Jewish history during the Second Temple period, see Josephus, *Jewish Antiquities*, Book IX–
XI (Cambridge, MA: Harvard University Press, 1956); Elias Bickerman, *From Ezra to the Host
of the Maccabees* (New York: Schocken Books, 1966); D.S. Russell, *Between the Testaments* (London: SCM Press, 1960).

4. On the history of Jerusalem during the Byzantine, Muslim, and Crusader eras, see Karen Arm-
strong, *Jerusalem: One City, Three Faiths* (New York: Ballantine Books, 1997).

5. On the history of the conflict over Jerusalem for biblical and modern times, see Dore Gold, *The
Fight for Jerusalem* (Washington, DC: Regnery Press, 2007).

Chapter 10: A Global Economy

1. Thomas Ice, "The Emerging Global Community," Pre-Trib Research Center, www.pre-trib.org/
articles/view/emerging-global-community.

2. Thomas Ice, "The Mark of the Beast," Pre-Trib Research Center, www.pre-trib.org/articles/view/
mark-of-beast.

3. Tim LaHaye, *Revelation Unveiled* (Grand Rapids: Zondervan, 1999), p. 227.

4. Thomas Ice, "The Late Great U.S.A." Pre-Trib Research Center, www.pre-trib.org/articles/view/
the-late-great-usa.

5. Mark Hitchcock, *The End of Money* (Eugene: Harvest House, 2009), p. 21.

6. Hitchcock, *The End of Money*, pp. 174-75.

Chapter 13: The Growth of the Church

1. John MacArthur, "Keys to Effective Evangelism, Part 1," *Grace to You*, www.gty.org/resources/study-guides/40-5167.

2. "A Response to ABC's the Search for Jesus," *The John Ankerberg Show*, 2001, cited in John Ankerberg and Dillon Burroughs, *What's the Big Deal About Jesus?* (Eugene: Harvest House, 2007), pp. 176-77.

3. Kenneth Latourette, *A History of Christianity* (London: Eyre & Spottiswoode), cited in William A. Dreyer, "The Growth of the Early Church," *HTS Teologiese Studies*, vol. 68, no. 1 (2012), www.hts.org.za/index.php/HTS/article/view/1268.

4. Bailey Smith, *Taking Back the Gospel* (Eugene: Harvest House, 1999), p. 8.

5. Warren Bird, "The World's Largest Churches," Leadership Network, leadnet.org/page/world?/world.

Chapter 14: The Spread of Evil

1. Leonard Blair, "Pastor Says 'Church Sucks,' Mixes Worship with Katy Perry, Maroon 5; Tells Congregation Not to 'Get Its Panties in a Bunch,'" *Christian Post*, September 24, 2013, www.christianpost.com/news/pastor-says-church-sucks-mixes-worship-with-katy-perry-maroon-5-tells-congregation-dont-get-your-panties-in-a-bunch-105212/.

A Final Word: How Tomorrow Impacts Today

1. This chapter is adapted from Ed Hindson and Tim LaHaye, "How Should We Then Live," chap. 15 in *Global Warning* (Eugene: Harvest House, 2007).

2. Erwin Lutzer, *Where Do We Go from Here?* (Chicago: Moody Press, 1993), pp. 25-48.

3. Bill Hybels, *Becoming a Contagious Christian* (Grand Rapids: Zondervan, 1994), pp. 43, 59.

4. Dave Hunt, *Whatever Happened to Heaven?* (Eugene: Harvest House, 1988), p. 7.

5. Joseph Stowell, "Set Your Mind on Heaven," in *10 Reasons Why Jesus Is Coming Soon* (Sisters, OR: Multnomah Books, 1998), p. 235.

6. C.S. Lewis, *Mere Christianity* (New York: Macmillan, 1943), p. 118.

7. Cited in Lutzer, *Where Do We Go from Here?* p. 46.

8. Cited in Lutzer, *Where Do We Go from Here?* p. 47.

9. John Walvoord, *Matthew: Thy Kingdom Come* (Chicago: Moody Press, 1974), p. 197.

ABOUT THE AUTHOR

Dr. Ed Hindson is assistant chancellor, dean of the school of religion, and distinguished professor of religion at Liberty University in Virginia. He also serves as the speaker on *The King Is Coming* worldwide telecast. In addition, Dr. Hindson serves as a visiting professor at the Veritas Evangelical Seminary in California, a board member of the Pre-Trib Research Center in Dallas, Texas, and a board member of the Hendley Foundation in Atlanta, Georgia.

Dr. Hindson holds graduate degrees from Trinity Evangelical Divinity School, Grace Theological Seminary, Trinity Graduate School, Westminster Theological Seminary, and the University of South Africa. He has written 40 books and more than 200 articles on a wide range of biblical, theological, and historical matters. He is coeditor of *The Popular Encyclopedia of Bible Prophecy, The Popular Encyclopedia of Apologetics,* and *The Popular Encyclopedia of Church History,* all published by Harvest House.

Dr. Hindson has lectured at more than 50 schools, including Oxford University and the Harvard Divinity School. He is a Life Fellow of the International Biographical Association (Cambridge, England) and has ministered extensively in North and South America, Europe, Asia, Africa, and Australia.

Ed and his wife, Donna, live in Forest, Virginia. They have three married children and seven grandchildren.

MORE GREAT
HARVEST HOUSE BOOKS
BY ED HINDSON

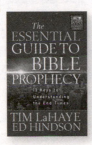

*The Essential Guide to
Bible Prophecy*
Tim LaHaye and Ed Hindson

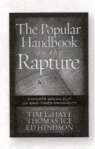

*The Popular Handbook
on the Rapture*
Tim LaHaye, Thomas Ice, and
Ed Hindson, general editors

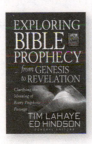

*Exploring Bible Prophecy from
Genesis to Revelation*
Tim LaHaye and Ed Hindson

*Trusting God When
Times Are Tough*
Ed Hindson

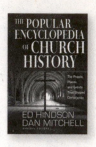

*The Popular Encyclopedia
of Apologetics*
Ed Hindson and Ergun Caner,
general editors

*The Popular Encyclopedia
of Church History*
Ed Hindson and Dan Mitchell,
general editors

*The Popular Encyclopedia of
Bible Prophecy*
Tim LaHaye and Ed Hindson,
general editors

Taking
Notes